The Art of Regenerative Educatorship

The Art of Regenerative Educatorship

A Developmental Guide

Mieke Lopes Cardozo

Bas van den Berg

Koen Wessels

Foreword by Ben Haggard

First published in 2025 by Amsterdam University Press Ltd.

Published 2025 by Routledge
4 Park Square, Milton Park, Abingdon, Oxon OX14 4RN
605 Third Avenue, New York, NY 10158

Routledge is an imprint of the Taylor & Francis Group, an informa business

© Authors / Taylor & Francis Group 2025

The Open Access version of this book, available at www.taylorfrancis.com, has been made available under a Creative Commons Attribution-NonCommercial-NoDerivatives (CC-BY- NC-ND) 4.0 International license.

Trademark notice: Product or corporate names may be trademarks or registered trademarks, and are used only for identification and explanation without intent to infringe.

ISBN: 9789048570522 (pbk)
ISBN: 9781003705321 (ebk)
NUR 100

Cover design : Matterhorn Amsterdam

Supported by Sofia Sarmiento

Developmentally edited by Nicholas Mang

With contributions in chapter 5 from Daan Buijs, Ingeborg Heezen, Michaela Hordijk, Alette Los, and Marlies van der Wee-Bedeker

DOI: 10.5117/9789048570522

For Product Safety Concerns and Information please contact our EU representative: GPSR@taylorandfrancis.com
Taylor & Francis Verlag GmbH, Kaufingerstraße 24, 80331 München, Germany

Contents

Foreword by Ben Haggard — 8

Glossary — 10

Introduction
An Emerging Regenerative Current in Education — 13
- A Dire Situation — 14
- A Regenerative Current — 16
- What We Set Out to Do in This Book — 19

Section 1
Storying Regenerative Education — 26

1 Opening Statements: From Existential Struggle to Regenerative Commitment — 30
- Koen's Opening Statement — 30
- Bas's Opening Statement — 32
- Mieke's Opening Statement — 35

Intermezzo
Intention Setting — 41

2 Learning with a Sense of Belonging — 42
- Introducing the Story — 42
- Imaging the story — 43
- A Deep Dive into the Story — 45
- Reflective Questions — 51
- Invitation to Disrupt Educational Relationships — 52

3 Guerrilla Gardening and Resourcing — 55
- Introducing the Story — 55
- Imaging the Story — 56
- Deep Dive into the Story — 59
- Reflective Questions — 67
- Invitation to be with the Law of Three — 68

| **4** | **Hospicing and Acupuncture** | **72** |

Introducing the Story — 72
Imaging the Story — 74
Deep Dive into the Story — 75
Reflective Questions — 81
Invitation to Ground and Let Go — 82

Section 2
Regenerative Educatorship — 86

| **5** | **Stepping into Regenerative Educatorship** | **88** |

Holding a Fireplace Conversation — 89

Our Fireplace Conversation — 91

The garden and the city — 91
Steadfastly coming from love — 92
To be an enlightening resource — 96
The mighty swan and the ugly duckling — 97
Collectively holding space — 99
Being in between — 102
Playfully going forth as constructive disruptors — 103

Intermezzo
Storying Your Own Regenerative Educatorship — 107

| **6** | **Thinking Regeneratively About Educatorship** | **109** |

Creating Systemic Frameworks — 110
Regenerative Paths – Journeying the Landscape of Regeneration — 111
Regenerative Virtues – Showing Up with Regenerative Intent — 113
Regenerative Capabilities – Stepping into Regenerative Action — 117

Intermezzo
Working with Regenerative Frameworks — 123

7   Closing Words: Gratefulness and Recommitments   127
   Letter by Mieke   127
   Letter by Bas   131
   Letter by Koen   132

Epilogue
The School of Regenerative Educators   136

Dedications and Acknowledgements   137

About the Authors and Co-creators   139

Testimonials   140

Foreword by Ben Haggard

The emerging field of regenerative development is experiencing a moment of rapid growth and evolution. Pioneering practitioners extend its underlying thinking technology into a wide variety of disciplines. Their work is based on fifty years of ongoing experimentation and practice in fields as diverse as agriculture, ecological planning, organizational transformation, and the design of human settlements and infrastructure. These pioneering efforts have yielded not only numerous practical examples, but also a field-tested body of theory. Out of this has come a proliferation of new experiments as the theory is adapted and evolved for application in investment and finance, philanthropy, international development, communications, governance, policy, community organizing, and Indigenous science, to name a few lines of inquiry.

One of the distinguishing characteristics of a regenerative approach is that it is inherently developmental. That is, even as it seeks to produce concrete results and to create change at a systems level, it also seeks to develop new capacity in the people, communities, organizations, and ecosystems that it touches. One could say that educating is at the heart of the regenerative enterprise, but not education as the term is usually applied. In the context of regeneration, education is understood to be the drawing out and cultivation of the innate potential and self-determination in all living systems, including humans. Implicit in this statement is that for education to be regenerative, it must be undertaken in ways that are consistent with regenerative principles and processes, all of which aim for alignment with the ways that living systems work.

The authors of this book have taken this imperative to heart, dedicating themselves to a journey of discovery regarding what regenerative education is and how it might be put into practice. Each of them is not only a professional educator, but also a thoughtful investigator into the underlying meaning, purposes, and potentialities of education. They have written a book that is charming, unorthodox, and faithful to the spirit of regenerative thought. They have not only shared with readers the results of their inquiries but have also made vivid the process by which these results were generated. It's a generous act, and it invites us to join them in their journey, testing their ideas within our own experience. I am grateful to be given the chance to follow along.

Ben Haggard
Principal and co-founding member of Regenesis Group
November 2024

Glossary

Regeneration is a living systems perspective on the development of socio-ecological systems and beings. Regeneration allows a system to realise more of its innate potential to foster the evolution of life within planetary boundaries. Regeneration is a life-giving process, organically creating healing and restoring balance. Regeneration is an evolutionary process inherent in life itself, which works to (re)direct trajectories of degenerative and/or depleted systems towards healthier and harmonious futures for all life involved. Regeneration is a cornerstone of the biological process of self-renewal and evolution of living systems. From a living systems theory of change perspective, regeneration of living systems encompasses humans, non-humans, and consciousness as part of nature.

Regenerative development refers to a system of developmental technologies and strategies that works to enhance the ability of living beings to co-evolve, so that the planet continues to express its potential for healthier systemic constellations through increased diversity, complexity, and creativity. A regenerative development theory of change moves beyond linear, problem-solving thinking and instead requires simultaneous development of inner and outer worlds, and of individual and collective capabilities, culture, and consciousness. Through this, regenerative development practitioners actively work on developing and manifesting lively images of whole living systems' innate potential to become more fully alive and to co-evolve with the larger wholes of which they are part. Such a potential-oriented and self-determining epistemology inspires a perspective on what a system could co-evolve towards and a deep-seated trust that this potential can be manifested.

Regenerative education refers to the systems of formal and informal education spaces, practices, rituals, ceremonies, and activities collectively inspired and sourced from regenerative beliefs, philosophies, and principles. Regenerative education is aimed at learning that emerges from and cares for the interconnected wellbeing and thriving of humans, non-humans, and ecosystems on Earth. Regenerative Education is seen as a co-evolutionary process among the people involved, including educators, learners, and the larger systems and communities in which these are nested. Regenerative education can emerge in the various interrelated contexts of human development and learning, which are located within the multiple levels of formal education systems, and in diverse non-formal developmental learning settings in communities or organisations.

Regenerative educatorship is the art and process of enlivening regeneration into education spaces and systems. It is the evolving practice of those who are energised by contributing to the potential of others to connect and engage with systemic and personal healing and flourishing. And it is the energy and ability that a practitioner brings forth to nurture the broader education systems in which they are nested. Since regenerative educatorship is directed both at the primary education process and at the communities, places and systems in which this is embedded, anyone working in education contexts can engage in it. Whether you're a teacher, a manager, a curriculum developer, a planner, or something else, you can play your part in the regeneration of education systems and practices. Regenerative educatorship is also not limited to institutes of formal education alone. There are many other arenas in which education processes unfold, such as museums, sport clubs, and community centres. These education arenas, too, can become increasingly regenerative through our collective efforts. Regenerative educatorship is a lifelong pursuit of the art and practice of nurturing human potential for co-evolution.

Regenerative school/university is a place of formal learning which aims to connect education to the potential of living systems. These places do so by committing their being to the regenerative potential of the places that they are embedded in and serve. They continuously strive towards mutual co-evolution towards finding ways of supporting people to develop healthier relationships with themselves, each other, and the world. They are places which foster learning communities that nurture a relational and nested-systems worldview characterised by love, presence, and courage.

Regenerative leadership is stewarding the art and processes of regeneration into working with systems. It is an evolving practice of anchoring, illuminating, and inspiring capacity development. The ability to provide a space for others to truly breathe and support their development of increasingly conscious states of being. To help others see the potential of themselves, their communities, and the systems they are nested in. Regenerative leaders act as stewards who shape the field to be conducive for the further reaching of the potential of the people and places around them. Often, they do this work in the background, hidden from sight – energised by a deep love, courage, and presence for what the living systems around them are and what they could become.

Resourcing, in the context of guiding someone as nested in their living systems, means committing to taking on the role and responsibility of offering/holding space for them to explore and develop their innate potential. Resourcing is not a service to be 'sold' or forced upon someone or a system but, rather, emerges from an intrinsically motivated request for regenerative resourcing support. Resourcing is distinctly different from advising – its purpose is not to tell a person, community, or organization what they should do, but to support them in building their innate capacity to see potential for co-evolution and to become more self-determined, creative, and effective in pursuing their vocation. Becoming a resource requires a continuous, possibly lifelong commitment to self-development and self-management. This means to *re-source* one's own states of energetic being, thinking and behaviour to increasingly become capable of deeply caring for other (non)humans' and systems' wellbeing and thriving. Resourcing requires committing to a healthy discipline in support of spiritual and body–mind consciousness and health in one's own living system, as part of essential inner work to show up appropriately and in service of the (non)humans and communities requesting resource support.

Imaging, which is different from imagining, is developing the discipline and capability to *see* living beings and systems *at work* in their nested place. When imaging a past, present, or future event or situation, we draw on our unique human capability to bring forth a living and experienced image – or inner movie – which reflects the essence and potential of what could become. With practice, imaging can support the development of an individual or collectively shared direction-point, or a so-called pole star, to build will and aspire regenerative efforts towards.

Introduction
An Emerging Regenerative Current in Education

Dear reader,

Welcome to this book. We – that is, Mieke, Bas, and Koen – hope that engaging with this book will be a wholesome, inspiring journey for you. Crafting it sure was for us.

This book arose from a deeply felt desire for education that truly serves the wellbeing and flourishing of all life: Of every 'student' or 'learner', each with their own biography, dreams, pains, obstacles, creativity, and potential. Of every place, each home to a unique and diverse community – people, animals, trees, plants, rivers, soil, etc. – living together in mutual interdependence. And of every educator, those courageous people who become more whole by offering themselves in service to the development of the potential of others. How can (non)formal education systems and practices help unfold this potential of all of us – human and more-than-human – to live meaningful and loving lives together? How can education form the cornerstone of a world in which we increasingly flourish with each other rather than at the cost of each other? These questions form the heart of *Regenerative Education*. Yet perhaps even more than being about regenerative education as a rich and diverse phenomenon, this book is about what we like to call *the Art of Regenerative Educatorship*[I], that is, the journey of educators of regenerating themselves, their practices, and the systems they are part of in pursuit of more life-affirming education potentialities. What does it mean, what does it take, and what is it like to move regeneratively with(in) contemporary learning spaces and connected societal (eco)systems? What obstacles and restraints might be part of a regenerative educator's path? What capacities do we need to nurture and develop along the way, and how can we do so together?

A Dire Situation

Of course, we cannot begin to consider these questions without acknowledging the dire situation we find ourselves in[2]. Yes, we are deeply worried about the ongoing destruction brought on the planet by a relatively small segment of humanity. The extent to which humanity extracts resources from our planet home and disrupts the wellbeing of ecosystems, all for the pursuit of economic growth, is absurd and dangerous. As we wrote the introduction to this book, we found ourselves on the lovely balcony of the Amsterdam home of Mieke. On this September day, it was 32 degrees C. It is obvious that a place like Amsterdam, towards the northern half of Europe, ought not to be so hot. It is projected that major cities in the Netherlands will have more than fifty so-called tropical heat days by 2050 on average annually[3]. Or consider what we've collectively done with and continue to do to the incredibly diverse and rich biological kingdom. So many species are no longer among us, and many others risk extinction within this century, due to our collective actions[4]. Yet other animals exist in such absurd numbers and in such dire conditions just to satisfy humanity's insatiable appetite. Libraries have been filled with books pointing at the moral failures and grave consequences of how we collectively abuse the Earth – our only home – and arguing for more just, inclusive, and sustainable economics, politics, societies, and lifestyles[5]. Yet ecological degeneration is still the dominant reality in today's world.

In many ways, all this goes hand in hand with societal and spiritual degeneration. So many people around the globe – more often than not people with a relatively small carbon footprint, and often people who are no stranger to social injustice in the first place – suffer from the consequences of climate collapse and collapsing political and economic systems. It's widely anticipated that this will only get worse, leading to new or increased refugee streams. Looking at current political debates and societal struggles around ongoing refugee crises, we fear what's to come. All the wars we continue to get caught up in together certainly do not help in this regard. Neither do the many ways in which polarisation, segregation, and social injustice continue to loom large within the borders of so many countries, including our own. If we truly take this all in, it's hardly surprising that so many people, and we count ourselves among them, experience (occasional) existential and spiritual distress living in today's world. Take for example the bizarre and unprecedented burnout and depression rates that we see in wealthy countries such as our own. Or consider the ongoing waves of protests against climate and social injustice, often led by young activists. These are clear indications that there is something missing, that being a rich country is not the same as being a thriving country[6]. So, how can we experience deep meaning, purpose, and connection in a world so full of injustice? A world still dominated by capitalism, consumerism, isolationism, patriarchism, and extractivism. A world in which it is so hard not to be addicted to the dopamine release of fast food, fast fashion, and a fast social life aided by the likes of TikTok and Tinder. A world, indeed, that easily feels shallow, doomed, and devoid of meaning. Amidst all this – and we are aware that there is much more that can be said about the dire state we're in – it is clear that humanity needs a story that unites rather than divides. A story that gives us courage and the means to remain, or become once more, committed to the wellbeing and thriving of ourselves, our communities, and the Earth. A story that helps us foster a deep sense of belonging in this world and to each other. A story of the potential for all to be(come) more fully alive, in mutuality. A story that enables us to take on the task that faces humanity – as regenerative scholar Daniel Wahl puts it, of 'redesigning the human presence on the Earth'[7].

Luckily, there is also much to draw hope from in these dire times. For example, there is hope in the adaptive capacity and the resiliency of nature, including humans. There are myriad examples of places that are recovering, restoring, and regenerating after collapse and calamity. Take, for example, the restoration of the Biesbosch nature reserve in the south-west of the Netherlands, which in the 1960s was so polluted there were no more fish and which is now home to more than a dozen different species of fish. Or the rights for nature movement, with its major successes in New Zealand and Europe[8]. Or the definitive action that humanity took to ban chlorofluorocarbons once it became apparent that they posed an existential threat to the ozone layer. There are myriad examples of small and global actions that have broadly made the world a healthier place. Of course, none of these changes were easy, and there are also myriad examples of changes that were attempted that have not (yet) manifested themselves. Yet to us, in our roles as educators, these examples of pioneering work feel like an invitation – or perhaps an urgent call. As educators who are committed to systems and practices of formal and informal education and human development, we live with the question of what role education can or should play in bringing about more regenerative futures. We have this strong, fundamental belief in the power of education, in education as a potential cornerstone of a thriving society for all. After all, where else in society could we spend so much effort on crafting our collective futures?

Seen from this deep-seated belief, we find it all the more painful to admit that education systems today are often themselves part of a degenerative state. Indeed, we must admit that it often feels to us as if our schools, colleges, and universities are heating – burning up their students, educators, and managers – as the Earth is heating up. We often feel disillusioned when witnessing our education systems' tendency to reproduce a competitive, neoliberal culture, in which teachers and students together run from test to test and learning tends to remain rather superficial and impersonal. We see an enormous challenge in the prevailing tendency in education policy to value uniform, measurable learning outcomes over diverse and unique trajectories of unfolding human potential – and in the tendency to value head over heart and to be blind to the unique stories, backgrounds, and needs of teachers and students alike. We feel an existential need to, in particular, cultivate a sense of love for and connection with the Earth and our communities, and to develop and express our own authentic ways to contribute. About thirty years ago, David Orr argued that a large part of our education systems and approaches contribute to the educating of more effective vandals of the Earth[9]. Contemporary critiques often echo this statement, arguing that education systems continue to reproduce forms of colonialism, extractivism, exclusion, and discrimination that many of us in them try so hard to move past[10]. To a large extent, in how we educate, we are still reproducing a story of separation, competition, and fragmentation, rather than co-creating a new, more fruitful story of interconnectedness, purpose, and potential.

A Regenerative Current

Despite the dire times we find ourselves in, and the complicity of education systems, we are far from desperate. The three of us wrote this book with a deep sense of hope and purpose seated in the potential of formal and non-formal education systems. For we do in fact experience ourselves to be part of the unfolding of another story that counteracts business as usual: the story of regeneration. Whilst working on this book, we have become increasingly aware that we are part of a growing current of regenerative thinking and acting that so many educators are ready to lean into. Educators who dare to do things differently. Educators who live the question: Whom do the earth, society, and the unique students I am privileged to work with truly call me to be(come) in this day and age? And, accordingly, educators who don't shy away from collaboratively disrupting and transforming programmes and systems to bring about more life-affirming education potentialities.

We want to highlight, at this point, that regenerative thinking is not specific to education [11]. As Ben Haggard alluded to in his foreword to this book, there are emerging chapters of the regenerative story in farming, business, design, architecture, and so forth. In all these contexts, regenerative agendas are sourced by a profound paradigmatic shift. A shift away from ways of thinking and acting that separate and evoke competition and zero-sum games, towards a worldview that emphasises interconnection[12]. Towards a fundamental commitment to the mutual wellbeing and thriving of humans, communities, and Earth. A commitment driven by a profound love and care about all life. At the same time, this awareness, commitment, love, and care are, of course, not new. There are numerous ancient wisdoms in which they hold a central role. To provide an example, we note that there's a conceptualisation in various Indigenous wisdom traditions of caring, of truly caring, through the notion of seven generations thinking[13]. Such perspectives encourage us to explore the 'inner dimensions' of regeneration – indeed, regeneration often begins with questioning our own patterns of thinking, feeling, and relating to the world – and can inspire us as we try to regenerate our contemporary education systems towards more life-affirming futures.

The emerging story of regeneration is one we'll explore throughout this book. But there is one core aim that regenerative practitioners seem to have in common – whether they're gardeners, farmers, architects, designers, educators, or something else – that we want to briefly mention at this point, namely, a steadfast commitment to see and sense potential, and to let it function as a pole star. Regenerative thinkers such as Carol Sanford, Ben Haggard, and Pamela Mang note how much of the work we usually do – for instance when working in education systems – takes place at what they call the level of existence. That is, work focused on increasing performance and efficiency of what is already there and finding solutions to problems that are experienced from within the current system or status quo. They contrast this with working in the realm of potential – the work that focuses on manifesting what could or wants to become. Within this realm of potential thinking, we can further distinguish between working on *improving systems* and on a *system-evolution approach to regeneration*: of revitalising a whole (learning) ecosystem in service of its further co-evolution[14].

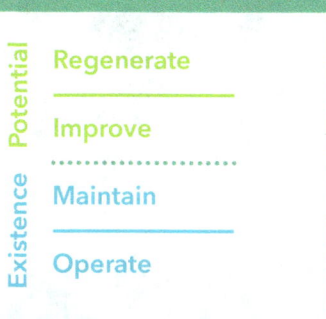

Figure 1: The Levels of Work (Mang and Reed, 2020:27).[15]

The Levels of Work (figure 1) is a fundamental framework of Regenerative Development. The framework helps us to consciously pause and reflect, both when we are in the midst of a pattern or practice that may not be reaching its regenerative potential and retrospectively. The four levels are a way of looking at patterns – recurring practices in systems, and finding ways to make them reach their potential. We are constantly moving through these levels, and one is not necessarily better than the other. For example, a non-operational hospital does none of its patients any good.

We discuss the framework, starting from the lower levels, then moving up. The realm of existence consists of two levels.
- Operate: When we are engaging at this level, we are not consciously working on changing the system. We are fully immersed in the activity as part of an ongoing, often automatic pattern. For example, when you are giving a class you have taught many times or when you are driving somewhere without fully consciously experiencing that you just did that.
- Maintain: When we are engaging at this level, we are conscious of what is required to keep a system going, and to adapt to changing circumstances. This could for example be thoughtfully including movement breaks into long meetings, including different modes of learning into a class, or adapting the contents and structure of a curriculum in response to external forces, such as political reforms or new pedagogical insights.

Please note that there may be moments when a system is in such a crisis, that even operating becomes impossible. The COVID-19 pandemic was a good example of this. But it can also be much smaller, for example if a serious conflict emerges between colleagues, students, or managers. It is likely that the situation is so destabilised that the first order of business is to restabilize it before you can work towards change. When a patient comes into the emergency room in the middle of a heart attack, you don't want the doctors to worry about the potential of the healthcare system. You want them to focus on saving the patient first.

Once we are able to go beyond maintaining, we reach the realm of potential.
- Improve: When we are engaging at this level, we are consciously trying to transform the way a system functions. Now, we are not just adapting to changing circumstances, we're actively creating new patterns that increase diversity, complexity, and creativity within the larger systems of which we are part. We are exploring longer-term possibilities to disrupt and innovate existing patterns. For instance, in chapter 4 you'll see Bas writing about his efforts to disrupt a pattern in contemporary education to lay emphasis on individual learning/performance through trying to create possibilities for 'group graduation' within his institute.
- Regenerate: When we are engaging at this level, we are working towards the long-term potential and evolution of a system. We are actively trying to foster a lively image of what a particular system – with its own unique essence and nestedness – can evolve into. And with this, we start to question how we should show up and collaborate to evoke a collective sense of direction, will, and capability to move towards such potential systemic constellations. When we reach this level, we start experiencing that we're in an emergent developmental conversation with each other, and that from this, the work we do on all the other levels (operate, maintain, improve) becomes more purposeful and aligned.

It may help here to think back on a work situation that you feel did not reach its full potential. Perhaps a class you taught or a meeting you were in. Or a research or teaching innovation project that you were involved in. Going through the Levels of Work, what becomes clear that you could not see before? When you get to the potential realm (improve and regenerate), you may ask: What could have manifested if I had tried to work from that level? We will ask you throughout this book to come back to this framework.

It is profoundly different to experience a problem and try to solve it than it is to sense a potential and serve its unfolding. The first is a story of stress and relief; the second is one of inspiration and actualization. Both are valid, both are needed. But it is in the attempt to stretch our thinking and acting to the scope of systemic potential that regeneration truly begins. This requires tapping into the essence of what systems may become and seeing how what we currently experience as big limitations and challenges might actually resolve once we shift our attention to nurturing the co-evolution of the whole systems that cause them in the first place[16]. If we dare listen, if we dare really connect, do we not find out that this potential is everywhere?

Inspired by our own engagements with regeneration and by the loving guidance of dear mentors, we have experienced that education indeed holds regenerative potential. It can foster and emancipate communities and help us connect with nature, each other, and ourselves. It can transform an experience of lack of meaning, purpose, or hope into an experience of vocation – a deep sense of what you've got to do in this world.[17] It can foster love, commitment, and courage, and thus create the conditions for peace, connection, and justice, rather than the conditions for polarisation, conflict, and war. In this belief, we are far from alone. There are so many beautiful examples of educators, schools, universities, and programs that pave the way for regenerative futures. We ourselves became increasingly aware of these when we joined forces with several other educator–researchers from various higher education institutes in the Netherlands in 2021 to form a Community of Practice Regenerative Education. With this group, we started exploring what shifts in education thinking and acting are involved in transforming our education systems and practices into more life-affirming ones. Our work on this book grew out of this, and we hope it'll strengthen and deepen the regenerative current in education.

What We Set Out to Do in This Book

We developed this book for the growing current of educators who are walking, or aspire to walk, down a path of regeneration. This book aims to resource you to dive deeper into your own teaching and the education systems you are nested within. It'll likely benefit your engagement with this book if you already have a base level of awareness of living systems thinking and regenerative development, but we have tried our best to make this book work for those for whom this is all rather new as well. If you're looking for a broader introduction into this field, we highly recommend engaging with the following resources: *Regenerative design and development*, by Nicholas Mang and Ben Haggard, from 2016; the works of Carol Sanford and Ben Haggard, especially *Indirect work* and *No more gold stars*, published in 2022 and 2023, respectively; and *Designing regenerative cultures*, by Daniel Wahl, released in 2016. You could also listen to The Regeneration Lab podcast series, available on all major podcast platforms.

In the chapters that follow, we share our collaborative journey of trying to understand and learn from some of our own efforts to create more regenerative education practices and systems. The story we tell is built up in two parts. In section 1, we share why/how we have become committed to regenerative education (chapter 1), and we take turns to help each other narrate and learn from recent education experiences.

We do so on three interwoven 'levels':
1. regeneration of educator–student relationships (chapter 2);
2. regeneration of education communities (chapter 3); and
3. moving regeneratively within education systems (chapter 4).

We want to highlight at the start of this book that our current lived experiences and immediate work contexts are most strongly situated in the (so-called) higher education arena. The examples we give and the stories we tell in this section thus mostly draw from these real lived experiences. Nevertheless, our intention and understanding is that much of what we witness and experience as educators in the context of universities reveals patterns that are recognizable throughout the whole of the education system. The diverse experiences we do have with research and change projects that engage primary, secondary, vocational, and community education strengthen us in this belief. If you work in a very different education context from the stories we share, we hope you can make the stories come alive in relation to your own place and experience. We are, in fact, very curious to find out over time what can be learned from this. Furthermore, we are testing the premise that working on our collective capabilities in regenerative educatorship is both relevant and urgent beyond formal education settings. Indeed, there are many settings beyond schools, colleges, and universities in which we can find and nurture learning spaces for humans to better understand and be part of uncertain, unfolding futures.

In section 2 of the book, it's harvest time. We start with a 'fireplace conversation' in which several members of the Dutch Community of Practice Regenerative Education join us in developing shared language and perspectives on what it means and asks of you to regenerate your own role(s) in the service of whole-system regeneration (chapter 5). We build on this rich conversation in chapter 6, in which we offer and narrate a set of dynamic frameworks that integrate the core capabilities and virtues for regenerative educatorship that emerged throughout this book. We finish by writing closing letters in which we reflect on our hopes and aspirations for this work and the broader regenerative current in education (chapter 7). Giving these hopes and aspirations concrete form, the epilogue of this book looks forward to the School of Regenerative Educators, which started to emerge concurrently with this book. In a way, this school is an escalating manifestation of this book, driven by a deep desire to work together with you on the local and global regeneration of education systems.

Throughout this book, we invite you to (continue to) embark on your own journey of regenerative educatorship. As you will encounter in this book, regenerative educatorship occurs concurrently along three pathways: the inner path, the communal path, and the living system path. We propose that working on creating change within the education system can only occur through nurturing communities of change and by personal transformation. For this reason, we start this book by diving into our inner paths, exploring the motivations that guided us along the path of regenerative educatorship. Whether this all feels very new to you or you've been walking this path for years, we would be honoured to be your companion and walk alongside you in this developmental journey. For this reason, you'll find intermezzos in this book as well as reflective questions at the end of several of the chapters. These have all been collated and designed to support you on your path. In doing so, we were inspired by regenerative scholar Daniel Wahl, who proposes that 'the greatest gift one can give and receive are better questions to live'. In addition, you will also encounter education inspirations where we share some of our own ways of working so that they may inform and inspire yours.

We would also like to mention that, through writing this book, we've been trying to experiment ourselves on how to craft a book on regenerative educatorship in a value-adding manner. We are testing through our work the premise that research, a crucial part of education and knowledge systems, can also be regenerative. To this end, we're happy to share that we did indeed experience writing this book as something different. In fact, we've made up a new word to describe how we've experienced our process: *existendipilation*. This word is a rather nerdy attempt to combine 'existential', 'serendipity', and 'escalation' into one new term. It stands for something like this: the experience when you start an activity and it makes you (collectively) stumble on rather existential questions, experiences, and insights, creating such an energy that the entire endeavour escalates until it becomes something beyond what you had initially imagined. That, at least, is our experience of writing this book, and we hope that engaging with it may have a similar effect on you. Whether it's about regenerative educatorship or doing regenerative research, or both, all three of us are happy to chat about avenues that may fit your explorations. More particularly, Bas is very susceptible to vegan pastries if you want to attract his attention. Koen loves hiking with his dog , and some human companionship whilst he's at it wouldn't hurt him, nor his dog[18]. And Mieke, well, she has made it her secret mission to spread her matcha-love as widely as possible, so just say you would love to try it (or treat her), and you're already best friends!

With that, let's get going!

Mieke, Bas, and Koen

"It is time now, and what a time to be alive

In this Great Turning we shall learn to lead in love"

We Shall Be Known, MaMuse, 2018

Notes

1. We follow the perspective that has been posited by, amongst others, Gert Biesta, when he described education at its finest as being a thoroughly practical art. Biesta, G. (2021). *World-centred education: A view for the present.* Routledge.
2. It is important to acknowledge that while we use the pronoun 'we' here, there are great differences both in persons' and nations' contributions to ecosystem disruption, as well as the local impacts of those disruptions. Indeed, those most at risk of climate collapse are often those who contributed the least to the collapse, which is a gross injustice.
3. In the context of Dutch policy making, these are days when the average temperature in the country exceeds 30 degrees C. Traditionally, these days have been rare (fewer than seven per year). While the Netherlands is a rich place and there is substantial scope for adaptation to this change, it is a certainty that this will cost (human) lives, especially of those who are already amongst the most marginalised in society.
4. The International Union for Conservation of Nature Red List, which monitors extinction (risk) for a wide array of species, indicates that more than 46,000 species are currently at (high) risk for extinction. For a vast majority of those, the risk is due to the way a relatively small percentage of humanity is (ab)using the Earth. At the same time, less than 3% of global mammalian biomass is wild animals – the remainder being humans and human-adjacent species such as dogs, cats, cattle, and farmed fish.
5. A good place to start for a historical exploration of this topic is Macintyre, T., Tilbury, D., & Wals, A. (2024). *Education and learning for sustainable futures – 50 years of learning for environment and change.* Routledge. While this book is written from the historical perspective of sustainability education, it provides a good overview of the broader environmental movement since the first UN summit for sustainable development in Stockholm, in 1972.
6. The rapidly emerging field of ecopsychology explores the interweaving of mental health (and thriving) and natural system health. For some introductory texts to the field, please check out Buzzell, L., & Chalquist, C. (2009). *Ecotherapy – Healing with nature in mind.* INGP; Roszek, T., Gomes, M.E., & Kanner, A.D. (1995). *Ecopsychology – Restoring the Earth, healing the mind.* Counterpoint LLC.
7. See Wahl, D. C. (2016). *Designing regenerative cultures.* Triarchy Press.

8   There are many examples of the rights of nature movement and their successes, and struggles, around the globe. The movement aims to instil 'personhood' to natural systems, such as river deltas, so that legally, it becomes much harder to exploit them. The most famous example is the Whanganui River system on the North Island of Aotearoa / New Zealand. These rights were granted in 2017 and established a council to oversee the (further) development of the river that is made up of representatives of different indigenous tribes and the New Zealand government. A rather good documentary about the impact of this decision on the river and local communities has been made named after a famous Maori saying: *I am the river and the river is me*, directed by Petr Lom.

9   See Orr, D. W. (1994). *Earth in mind - On education, environment and the human prospect.* Island Pr.

10 While there are many great thinkers out there reflecting on the structural 'wrongs' of education systems in the past, present, and future, we feel that the works of Sriprakash (2023) and Zembylas (2017) are especially relevant in relation to waking up and rethinking and reshaping ways in which we envision and engage with education systems meaningfully, through material, epistemic, and pedagogical/relational reparations, to truly work on more just education futures. Zembylas, M. (2017). Love as ethico-political practice: Inventing reparative pedagogies of aimance in 'disjointed' times. *Journal of Curriculum and Pedagogy, 14*(1), 23-38. DOI 10.1080/15505170.2016.1277572. Sriprakash, A. (2023). Reparations: theorising just futures of education. *Discourse: Studies in the Cultural Politics of Education, 44*(5), 782-795. DOI: 10.1080/01596306.2022.2144141.

11 There exists a long lineage of regenerative scholars who have been trying to create movement for more life-affirming possibilities for a long time. Recently, Belgian colleagues (Gorissen et al. 2024) wrote a report that provides an accessible overview of some of the ways that the regenerative field has been developing. In this book, we engage most strongly with two lineages of regenerative thinking: 1) the lineage of the regenerative development field, and particularly the rich contributions hereto of the Regenesis Institute (Mang & Haggard, 2016); and 2) the lineage of the regenerative design field (e.g. Wahl, 2016; Lyle, 1992). Gorissen, L., Bonaldi, K., Haerens, P., & Rato, L. (2024). *Regenerative development and design: Its origin, essence, practice and potential as a meta-discipline to elevate governance, innovation and planetary health.* FPS Public Health. Mang, P., & Haggard, B. (2016). *Regenerative development: A framework for evolving sustainability.* Wiley. Wahl, D.C. (2016). *Designing regenerative cultures.* Triarchy Press. Lyle, J.T. (1992). *Regenerative design for sustainable development.* Wiley.

12   This is often described as a turn towards relational ontology that is inherent in living systems thinking. Koen's doctoral dissertation offers an exploration of such a turn in the context of education philosophy. Wessels, K. R. (2022). Pedagogy of entanglement: A response to the complex challenges of our time. Springer.

13   While these traditions are ancient, they came to the fore of the Westernised canon when introduced in the report by Clarkson et al. (1992). This is an approach to communal decision making that incorporates the perspectives of seven generations of ancestors and descendants for choices made now. In their recent book, Carol Sanford and Ben Haggard (2022) use this notion to explore how expanding our scope of consciousness is crucial for processes of regeneration. It seems to us that this way of thinking about 'inner work' is gaining traction today. Perhaps the best example hereof is the emergence of the so-called Inner Development Goals, led by an international consortium based out of Stockholm, as an attempt to complement the Sustainable Development Goals to arrive at a more holistic approach. Clarkson, L., Morissette, V., & Régallet, G. (1992). *Our responsibility to the seventh generation: Indigenous peoples and sustainable development.* IISD. Sanford, C., & Haggard, B. (2022). *Indirect work: A regenerative change theory for businesses, communities, institutions and humans.* InterOctave Inc.

14   Inspired by our training with Ben Haggard, Pamela Mang, and Carol Sanford, we refer here to a framework called Levels of work, initially developed by their mentor Charles Krone. *Levels of Work* © 1984 by Charles Krone Associates is licensed under CC BY-SA 4.0. To view a copy of this license, visit http://creativecommons.org/licenses/by-sa/4.0/.

15   Mang, P., & Reed, B. (2020). Regenerative development and design. In R. Meyers (Ed.), *Encyclopedia of sustainability science and technology* (2nd edition, pp. 115–142). Springer.

16   Sanford, C., & Haggard, B. (2023). *No more gold stars: Regenerating capacity to think for ourselves.* Intercotave.

17   Here, we find inspiration in the work of spiritual education scholar Parker Palmer to 'listen for the voice of vocation'; see Palmer, P. (2000). *Let your life speak: Listening for the voice of vocation.* Jossey-Bass; (1997). *The courage to teach: Exploring the inner landscape of a teacher's life.* Jossey-Bass.

18   Note from Bas: Just make sure you are prepared for big dog hugs.

Section 1

Storying Regenerative Education

Now that we've welcomed you into this book, let us embark on a journey together! In the four chapters that follow as part of section 1 of the book, we welcome you into our unfolding stories of trying to regenerate the education systems and practices that the three of us find ourselves engaged with. These stories are specific, contextualised, and unique, and they include our moments of insight and wonder just as much as our missteps and vulnerabilities. They do not offer instructions or methods that can be blindly copied to other contexts; we share them because they hold the potential to trigger reflections for other education stories. Every story of regeneration is unique, yet if we look closely, the stories all illuminate elements of the larger regenerative narrative.

This section contains four chapters that build on each other. In chapter 1, we each share a personal opening statement[1]. Whereas in the preface we painted a generic picture of the regenerative commitments of this book, we now reveal some core elements of how, and why, we personally feel the path of regenerative educatorship is one we're called to walk. In doing so, we start engaging with some of the central themes of this book – such as love, healing, courage, pain, community, belonging, and presence – in an intimate way. We want to emphasise that our opening statements might contain elements that touch upon painful or traumatic experiences in your own life. For instance, themes such as illness, suicide, social exclusion, and war are present in our stories, and in many ways it's the processes of healing from these challenges that underly our hopeful and passionate commitment to regenerative education.

Starting this book in this personal way is a conscious and philosophical choice, as it positions the existential journey of individual beings at the heart of processes of collective inquiry and systemic change. We explicitly want to convey the message that everyone's unique stories matter, and that inner transformation and system change go hand in hand. In a more practical sense, we also share these personal statements to add depth to the education stories we'll tell next, as the way we each show up in and talk about our work as educators has deep roots in our evolving autobiographies.

In chapters 2–4, we move on to collaboratively dive into some of our unique stories of trying to fulfil more regenerative education potentialities. In each chapter, we zoom in on one story, introduced by one of us, and focusing on a particular education relationship. First, Koen introduces a story about regenerating our relationship with students (chapter 2), before Mieke does the same for our relationship with our fellow educators (chapter 3), and Bas for the way we relate to institute/system dynamics (chapter 4). These three chapters are adapted versions of recorded conversations, and we've chosen to present them to you as conversations. You'll see that in these conversations we have worked with two 'roles', the roles of 'story shaper' – i.e. the person bringing in and developing a story – and the role of 'resource'. As a resource, one's task is to full-heartedly support the story shaper, by actively listening and by being available to offer support when asked or intuitively prompted, for instance by asking open-ended questions and/or mindfully sharing observations, experiences, or perspectives to elucidate the full richness of the story being developed. We are committed to develop our internal capabilities to develop appropriate and developmental questions, which we often source from regenerative framework thinking. With these roles, we further structured each conversation along three steps. The first step is that the story shaper provides a brief introduction of the context and central themes of a story. The second step is that we each individually engage in an imaging exercise in which we allow ourselves to let the story come alive to us in a unique, creative, and dynamic way (for more clarity on what imaging is, see the glossary or the textbox 'An imaging exercise', in chapter 2). After sharing our imaging with each other, we follow with a third step, in which we engage in a deeper explorative conversation to develop the central themes and perspectives of the story.

Notes

1. The first thing we did when we started working on this book was to each write a letter to the other two in which we shared our personal stories as to how and why we became so invested in regenerative education to begin with. Doing so created the energy and shared commitment we needed to write this book the way we did, and the only way we could: as a regenerative journey in and of itself. The statements we share here are an adapted version of these initial letters we wrote to each other.

2. Methodologically, these steps are a combination of micro-phenomenology (see the work of Claire Petitmengin) and collective autoethnography (see the work of T.K. Noel and colleagues (2023), as well as the life work of Arthur Bochner and Carolyn Ellis as a way of both helping each other formulate their own narratives, but to do so in an explicitly nested way with larger education system themes and patterns. As will become clearer in the latter part of this book, our approach is further inspired by regenerative dynamic living system frameworks from the tradition of the Regenesis Institute and the work of Carol Sanford. Noel, T.K., Minematsu, A., & Bosca, N. (2023). Collective Autoethnography as Transformative Narrative Methodology. *International Journal of Qualitative Methods*, 22. DOI 10.1177/16094069231203944

1 Opening Statements: From Existential Struggle to Regenerative Commitment

Koen's Opening Statement

The question I want to bring in at the start of this book is this: What does it mean truly to belong? To belong to a group, a family, a job, a community, an ecosystem? To be at home here on Earth? I sure haven't got a final answer myself, but actively living with this question for years now is what made me end up sitting behind my laptop to write this opening statement.

Among my own most vivid early life experiences are confrontations with quite the opposite of belonging. When I was 8 years old, my father's sister ended her own life, and when I was 14 years old, my mother's sister did the same. Both had their own unique stories. And the highs and lows of my mother's sister in particular played a big part in our family as I was growing up. Having witnessed both my aunts arrive at a point where they saw no way forward to belong here on Earth, and having been a son of parents confronted with this fact, has, for sure, been a powerful trigger for me.

In my own way, I, too, have experienced emotions and states of mind that put my sense of belonging here on Earth at risk. I have experienced, and often still do, a strong anger, frustration, disgust, and fear regarding the atrocities humans are capable of, both on small and on large scales. Why do people bully each other? How dare someone knowingly skip the line at the bakery or airport? Why do we wage wars? How could we possibly be so cruel as to invent slavery? To colonise and conquer? To kill entire species of precious animals? To invent policies and install bureaucracies that systematically disregard human dignity? I've discovered that confrontation with such destructive forces in our world tends to trigger a retractive response in me, a response that essentially communicates: 'The world sucks, people suck; I'll just step away, be angry from a distance, and feel superior'. And I've come to understand that this response essentially opens the door to the extreme point of view that this world is, in fact, not worth belonging to. Against my family background, it is, perhaps, not surprising that as I grew older, I started to feel a strong need to resist such a nihilistic, fatalistic outlook. In my own way I've come to understand that there is another, more desirable path to walk. A regenerative path, a path of belonging. A path of not retracting and opposing myself but of engaging from a position of caring and love. A path of challenging myself to look deeper into the origin of destructive forces and behaviour – both in myself and in others. A path of seeing the beauty and potential inherent in all life. And a path of humbly trying to find my own way to give or create something that matters and is sincere. Walking this path is, indeed, a lifelong quest. A path that continues to require regeneration of how we think and show up in the world. I think it's a dedication to do so that brings us together in books like this. We all have our own ways of slipping into degenerative modes of thinking and being, but we also all have a deep existential longing to live regenerative lives, and to experience a deep sense of belonging. Of this I am convinced.

There is another thread that I'd like to weave into my opening statement. A thread that has to do with another unanticipated part of my biography, which has opened my eyes regarding the question of belonging. When I was about to turn 20, I fell desperately in love with a Turkish woman as I was travelling in the south of Spain. This turned out to be the beginning of a long-distance relationship, with me moving to Istanbul and, later, her coming to live in the Netherlands. As I often jokingly put it: Ours is a holiday love that just keeps on escalating. But the story I want to tell here is not about our relationship as such, but about how it has allowed me to start belonging to a second country: Türkiye. Learning the Turkish language, living in Türkiye, becoming part of my partner's family and circles of friends is a gift that keeps on giving. It's made me reflect on my own upbringing, relationships, and culture, and together my partner and I are caught up in this great adventure of weaving our cultures together into something new. Now, what this boils down to, for me, is that we're in a process of overcoming the 'individualism–collectivism split' that is so prevalent in contemporary society. This notion that a person, or a culture, is focused either more on individual development, freedom, and expression *or* more on collective identity, unity, and service. You know, I've come to deeply value the space for self-exploration and the celebration of authenticity that I've been brought up with, and in many ways I experience more freedom and possibility in the Netherlands than I do in Türkiye. Yet every time I set foot in Türkiye, I feel like I'm coming home amidst warm and strong friendship and family bonds, and the expressions of hospitality and care for strangers as well as stray cats and dogs that I witness all around. This dual reality has made one thing so obviously self-evident for me that I want to scream it off every roof: A happy, flourishing life is not about self-absorbed self-development, nor about serving something larger than oneself without considering how you personally fit into it all. It's about serving the concrete places and lives you are part of in ways that belong to you. It's in transforming and expressing our own unique stories and voices in service of the places and beings we love, that our chests burst with life.

Selfhood and service are not opposites. They are two sides of one and the same experience of being whole. Of living a life full of love. Of belonging. That's the main lesson my life has been teaching me so far, and every fibre in my body tells me that we need this awareness more than ever to collectively navigate these messy times we live in. Saving the world from looming socio-ecological collapse feels like far too heavy a load to carry. But finding my way to love the world, to develop and express my potential in service of it, to listen carefully for ways in which I can, and feel inspired to, make a difference that matters; that I can do. We do not need a perfect world to belong in it. We simply need to love ourselves and those around us, and then act in service of what we love. This is not rocket science. But it does take a lot of will, consciousness, and nurturing. It asks – indeed – for regenerative education.

For me personally, all of the above is stuff I've been figuring out despite, rather than thanks to, formal education. Only on rare occasions have I experienced that formal education nurtured a sense of intimate relationship with nature, myself, fellow students, teachers, or community. And only rarely have I truly felt supported to explore and regenerate my own unique way of showing up in and contributing to the places and communities I am part of. Don't get me wrong: I have found plenty of teachers and inspiring learning spaces in my life, just more often out of school than in it. And that feels like such a shame, such a waste of potential. This, I sense, is an experience that so many of us – and perhaps you, too – share. The stories in this book, and the perspectives developed along the way, show how very different it can be.

Bas's Opening Statement

It is impossible for me not to be moved by Koen's words. I also, often, have felt that I do not belong in this world. Perhaps it is more honest to say that I have felt that the world deserved better. Not better just from me necessarily, but better from us all. I have never understood why we would cut through the forests, empty rivers and seas from fish and disrupt the land with careless abandon, as if the living things on the little blue ball in the middle of the Milky Way galaxy we call home are not conscious or do not matter. At times, I have felt so disconnected that I thought that continuing to live was no longer a viable path for me. I have luckily, and gratefully, been able to receive help every time I had one of these bouts. Finding this regenerative path, and sensing all the enthusiasm that I encounter from others along the way, is one of the key bedrocks in my life. It is interesting how something can simultaneously act as a pole star, meaning something we aspire towards, and as a bedrock, meaning something that provides a solid foundation. Yet, with regeneration that is the case for me. Living the regenerative potential of education spaces provides me with an avenue to find purpose and connection in this world, despite the dire situation we're in. The pursuit of this path opens questions that I hold close to my heart, and which play a central role in the professorship that I currently hold, as well as in the rest of my life[1].

For this book, I will open my heart and share these questions with you. The main question I am holding as we step into the crafting of this work is the following: What does it mean to transform pain and suffering into regeneration? What does it require from us to look in the depths of collapse and use these depths as a resource to make the world a more beautiful and healthier place? How can we make sure that we stay in love with life, even when that seems unbearable? It is a question that is relevant for me for a multitude of reasons. You see, for the last nine years, eight months, and twenty-two days (at the moment of redrafting this opening statement, in November 2024) I have lived with unrelenting pain. During the co-writing of this work, I also struggled with a bout of depression, which included passive suicidal ideation that required intensive medical care. You see, it is not easy to live on this planet when the body that you inhabit feels as sick as the Earth sometimes seems to be. Indeed, working on this book with Koen and Mieke has played a big part in my ability to recover.

When the pain from my disease started, I had a choice. I could either let the pain take over and become a bitter man. Or I could try to channel it into something that was worth supporting. Through the work of Daniel Wahl, I encountered the regenerative movement[2]. With his loving encouragement, as well as those of others, such as my PhD supervisors, I began walking down the path I am currently still on. A path of being with the questions that I just posed. A path of asking these questions within/with education systems, educators, and education practice. A path of trying to contribute to more life-aligned education, where some of the central themes of this book, such as pain, suffering, love, and courage, could play a role, became my way of transforming the energy that was eating up my body into something I could be proud of. There was no way to imagine how my 'body of work' has unfolded since then. Now, there are dozens of educators across different countries who are exploring regenerative approaches to their education practices. They are all, in their own way, asking questions that disrupt, through love, the way education tends to work.

What if, for example, we see it as the purpose of education to look at the injustices in the world, those all around us, such as (energy) poverty or animal rights abuses, and to empower students and teachers alike to transform them? What if, for example, it becomes normalised to bring your whole self into education spaces, spaces that are supportive of emotions and feelings? What if we look at education places as spaces where we can contribute to the healing of society and the Earth? These are questions many educators are living today. Brave educators, courageously going where no one has gone before. Of course, the dual development of self and the Earth play a key role here. Everything we do touches the world, and in every touch that we make we are also touched. But what if we stopped and listened, instead of bulldozing our way through the boundaries of the Earth, our societies, and our own bodies? Admittedly, I am not particularly good at the last of these yet. There are many challenges about learning to live with a disability that are akin to learning to live on a planet that is, in some ways, being disabled. Among these is that your limits are sharper and more frustrating. It is not easy or fun to not be able to do something (anymore). Yet, it is one of the key things that all of us will need to learn if we are to truly redesign our presence on the Earth. Trust me, I know it's hard.

In this book, I will talk about the challenges of these limits and boundaries further. Regeneration is based on the flows and rhythms of natural systems. It is important to highlight that natural systems have limits, and that they require death, decay, and, indeed, pain. They are, in some ways, the key ingredients for further evolution. The ability to develop further is often paved by the bodies of those who came before you. Just like I will one day return to the ground, many of the education practices that have become dominant in regard to assessment, didactics, pedagogies, and management must be hospiced. They must be lovingly supported in their dying, for it is in their final breaths that space for new potential emerges. One of the key challenges that regenerative educators face is precisely the art of learning to let go. Or, to make sure you are always holding onto things lightly enough that you can move beyond them when it becomes necessary for the greater whole. I have been lucky enough to experience great examples of grace and elegance in the face of decay and decline. I know that is a rare privilege indeed. Most of us are terrified of looking finality in the eye. We gasp for air and hold on for every single second, fighting against the inevitable. My old Judo sensei did not do that. He taught until he was well into his late eighties, yet he adapted. He was long past the physical prowess to throw or be thrown. He was able to use his students as examples to continue his teachings. My very first introduction to educatorship was through his resilience. He showed me you can still be courageous, loving, and present, even when you are in the midst of your personal decay. He showed me you can still be an educator at the very edges of life. I am forever grateful for this lesson. Because in many ways, all educators are moving towards that edge as we continue to push ecosystems out of balance. Stepping towards that edge and peaking over, let alone to take a stand there or move along the edge, is potentially petrifying. Yet, I posit, it is exactly what this education moment is demanding from us. Standing on that knife's edge is exactly what the Earth requires from us.

This book, from my perspective, engages with how all of us can collectively do so. How can we find the courage to balance on those edges? How can we (re-)source ourselves and others with love for the potential of life on Earth? And how can we do so with the attention that this education movement asks of us? I hope that this book may help in acting as a bedrock and a pole star. It may not seem like it, but I am fundamentally someone with a positive outlook on life and on humanity. It is this faith, in the potential of education, that helps me transform my pain into action. If you are like me, education continues to be a lifeline in re-finding purpose in the face of the dire situation of the Earth.

I have spoken in the past about the lived sense of guilt and shame that I experience living with a disability. It hurts my soul when I must ask for special accommodations or feel like I am a drag on society, my colleagues, or my students. I live with the feeling right now that – as a species – we are collectively a burden on the planet. For me, regenerative education is walking towards a path where education can intentionally transform our burden-ness towards a more giving and caring relationship with each other and the rest of life. It is about finding ways of transforming our collective pains and sufferings into healing for ourselves, our communities, and the living systems we are expressions off. In this book, we will highlight several ways that we have gone about doing this work – the work that is the vocation of our lives. The work is not over, nor can it ever truly be.

Mieke's Opening Statement

As I am letting the personal and touching opening statements of Koen and Bas sink in, I feel invited – and encouraged – to open up to an inner dive myself. In this unfolding journey of exploring what becoming a regenerative educator means in my life story so far, it feels not just appropriate, but actually really crucial to take the time to engage with some of the more existential questions. And to become more attentive to the deeply felt intrinsic motivations which shape who I am today – and to what drives and supports me in my work and my engagements in the world.

My parents tell me how as a young girl, I expressed a deep interest in stories about war, peace, and resistance. Starting when I was nine, they often found me in our horse Sandra's stable or meadow, reading a book in her company, mostly filled with historical narratives about (world) wars[4]. Looking back, my fascination with stories about war and peace was likely nourished by the slowly unfolding – to me at least – (his)story of both my father's and my mother's side of my family, from whom I carry the genes of two remarkably strong-willed great-grandmothers. About a year ago, after many years of hesitation, I finally found the courage to start connecting with my family tree and my ancestors' stories, by working with my reiki master Rebecca Bredenhof in a Healing Your Family Tree course. Becoming a mother of twins in 2018, quite an existential journey in itself, gave me the sense of responsibility to break with silences, explore untold stories, and, in doing so, heal their effects in my own life, and for future generations.

Although I and my brothers carry my father's originally Portuguese Jewish surname, Lopes Cardozo, I did not know much about the roots of that name until I was about 9 years old. My paternal grandmother, Masha Raismann, a Jew originally from Russia, had broken with the Jewish community by 1907, and she consciously raised her children, including my grandfather, without ties to the Jewish religious community. Nonetheless she still had to flee and seek hiding during the war, while my great-grandfather Ben Lopes Cardozo resisted the Nazi regimes' requirement to wear a Jew star in his own way, by committing suicide on the night before this became obligatory. My paternal grandfather Max survived the war in a camp for prisoners of war as an army officer, yet he hardly spoke about his experiences or those of his parents and siblings to his children, or to us grandchildren.

Silenced stories and traumas related to otherness and war also play a role on my mother's side of my family tree. As a teenager and young adult, I witnessed how part of our family history became a public one, named Sonny Boy.

> "When there are grey skies
> I don't mind grey skies
> You make them blue, Sonny Boy"
>
> *Ray Henderson, Buddy De Sylva, and Lew Brown, 'Sonny Boy'*

Sonny Boy was the nickname given to my half Dutch–half Surinamese great-uncle on my mother's side of the family, Waldy Nods, and it is the name of the biographical novel which tells the powerful and heartbreaking story of my maternal great-grandmother Rika van der Lans and her complicated and forbidden love stories before and during the Second World War[5]. In a tiny nutshell, my great-grandmother's life was characterised by choosing love over religious or cultural expectations, with a first marriage across religiously segregated Catholic and Protestant communities, and a second marriage with a black, Surinamese, 17-year-younger husband, Waldemar Nods – with whom she supported the resistance movement and the hiding of Jews in their home during the Second World War. The public revealing of this story has been experienced as painful by a part of our family. I am personally deeply grateful that my ancestors' incredible courage and difficult struggles and life endings were brought to the surface by the author Annejet van der Zijl, and over the past decades have become part of a collective Dutch literary memory.

My deep dive into family tree work, in combination with my commitment to regenerative thinking and development in my various roles in life, is slowly allowing me to become more fully present to understand, interpret, and work with my personal drives, fears, and hopes. With my parents and brothers, I can now reflect on the family silences they have experienced around stories connected to the war, to complicated religious identifications, to resistance and discrimination. I am grateful that in my upbringing, these silences around family stories and traumas were slowly opening up, and how I felt encouraged to develop my curiosity in these themes as a student and, later on, as a researcher and–educator. The tragic life stories and tragic deaths of my ancestors thus find continued aliveness in my own unfolding life story. Mustering the courage and taking the time to deep dive into my family history also allows me to retrospectively understand more about how my education journey has at times felt, well, complicated.

School, for me, was a place where I experienced the joy of learning, yet also a place where I started to experience a sense of 'otherness'. My surname, as well as our way of speaking (which was not the local dialect), were at times the ingredients to be called out by other kids as an 'import', and for being different. I vividly remember how one day at school when I was about 9 years old, I was being called 'vieze *Jude*' (dirty Jew, using the German word for Jew) in the school playing ground. Without knowing the meaning of the word *Jude*, I felt deeply distressed and cycled home in tears, where my father was waiting for me with lunch. He used this moment to tell me more about the story of our family name, our ancestors' religious identities, and the history of the persecution of Jews during the Second World War. It slowly made me realise how the use of '*Jude*' as a term of abuse by kids in the school playground was likely informed by the way their parents spoke of us, and the local history of national-socialism and fascism, which was quite present in the village we lived in at that time. As I grew older, what my father told me made me realise how only a few decades ago, with our surname, we would have lived in a very challenging and even dangerous situation – and how the teaching of history in school did little to reconcile (with) such historical events and injustices.

Such experiences prepared the ground for my understanding that, on the one hand, schools can be places which generate a sense of belonging and invite a drive to develop and learn and, on the other hand, schools can also become alienating, exclusionary, and motivation-dampening environments – and even places where silences about past injustices were being (un)consciously reproduced. This understanding informed by personal education experiences, inspired a deep desire and strong drive to focus my studies and work on what we humans have come to term our 'education systems' – and how these intersect with stories and questions about war, peace, and (in)justices. It led me into my work in academia and to becoming an educator and researcher focused on peace education.

Both as a university student and, later on, as a developing scholar, I experienced how the pressures and pace of academia quite literally caused pain in my body. Two decades ago I started practicing yoga and soon after reiki, as a way to deal with the pain of an autoimmune reaction in my digestive system. Retrospectively, I now see how these spiritual and body–mind wisdom traditions and practices have made it possible for me to not drop out of academia but, instead, find ways to mitigate the overheating impact it was – and often still is – having on me. When I finished my PhD, in 2011, my wish list for gifts from family and friends at the post-defense party consisted of a contribution to do a yoga teacher training. In the years after, before mindfulness or contemplative practices became somewhat more welcomed in Dutch university life, I started integrating yogic ways of learning and being into my role as an educator in university, often wondering if I might somehow lose credibility or career perspectives in doing so. In 2015, I was introduced into what I now consider a mind-blowing, eye-opening, and heart-opening learning experience, of a regenerative development training. This invitation would soon turn upside down my entire outlook on my role as academic scholar, as educator, and as citizen and, later on, as mother. And it came from an unexpected direction, as this training was offered by Ben Haggard in reiki Centre Zijn (*tr.* to be) in The Hague, where my reiki master Rebecca Bredenhof lives and works. It was a place which I mostly connected with my personal path of healing and wellbeing, and not directly with my professional development. Little did I know!

By now, a regenerative paradigm for living and being is inspiring all my different roles in life, from parent to partner, from educator to researcher, from citizen to community engager, from friend to family member. Developing my capabilities as a regenerative thinker and practitioner has given me the courage to step into pioneering roles ahead of the curve, even when (or perhaps especially when) these feel scary and challenging, including consciously integrating the spiritual traditions of yogic and reiki practices and philosophy into academic work. It has given me the courage to say yes to unusual and untraditional twists and turns in my career, by slowly letting go of the increasingly uncomfortable role of (European, white) international peacebuilding education expert in conflict-affected regions, and instead build more co-creative partnerships with colleagues within and outside of the Netherlands and within and outside of academia, including collaborating with theatre groups. Working together, including as part of this book writing process with Koen and Bas, and being embedded in several regenerative communities and collaborations, is giving me the courage to take this deep dive into the vulnerability of exploring the deeper and intergenerational roots which belong to my story, and which inform who I am called to be in the world.

Our three opening statements are a testimony to a shared vocation to explore the potential of a regenerative understanding of and approach to education. We are very curious to see where our shared journey – in engagement with the wisdom and curiosity of our readers – will lead us in evolving our understanding of what 'regenerative education' can be(come). Let's surf those waves!

"Not all those who wander are lost"

J.R.R. Tolkien, *The Fellowship of the Ring*

Notes

1. Co-currently with the work in this book, Bas has been working on a series of short novels which engage with the following central themes and questions: (1) Acceptance: How can I learn to live with a reality that is no longer sustainable? (2) Resilience: How can I refind my path when I have lost the way? and (3) Steadfastness: How can I stay true to my path when the forces around me wish me to falter? This trilogy of novels further builds on the auto-ethnographic approach presented in this book and combines it with the concept of social fiction as proposed by Patricia Leavy. See, e.g., Leavy, P. (2022). *Re/invention – Methods of social fiction.* Guildford Press). Bas would not have found the courage to do this without having gone on the journey of co-crafting this book with Koen and Mieke.
2. Daniel and Bas recorded an episode about regenerative education for The Regeneration Lab podcast in 2021, available on all major platforms. See https://open.spotify.com/episode/09kpkNlFBht2s1hzT5Rc6F?si=hsiXKRgfRpu4Jtdzjnq35Q
3. For a deeper engagement with this lived sense of guilt, see also the third chapter of Van den Berg, B. (2023). *Design principles for regenerative higher education in times of sustainability transitions.* Wageningen University & Research.
4. The love for our horse Sandra was captured when I was 12 by photographer, writer, and dear family member Tom Weerheijm, my uncle Dick Lopes Cardozo's life partner, in his 1998 book *Honderduit – Eén eeuw vrouwen in woord en beeld.* Kwadraat Non Fictie.
5. Van der Zijl, A. (2004). *Sonny Boy.* Hollands Diep.

Intermezzo
Intention Setting

If you picked up this book, you probably have similar concerns about the world as we do. It's likely that, in your own way, you, too, resist an outlook on life and society that emphasizes individual gain at the cost of others and the Earth – that you look at life, or at least try to, in terms of mutuality, diversity, connection, and potential. Perhaps you're familiar with living systems thinking or regenerative thinking, or perhaps you have an intimate relationship to another particular holistic practice. And maybe you're already walking a path of purposefully approaching education processes and systems through these lenses or practices. Wherever you are on your path, we hope this book can be of service to its unfolding.

In the introduction and in our opening statements, we've tried to set the stage for the explorations that follow in the next chapters. We've introduced the emerging regenerative current in education and showed how our own unfolding paths are part of it. In this intermezzo, we'd like to invite you to do the same. And with that, to set your intention and energy for engaging with this book. You see, this book is in a way an unfinished product. It's only through you – our dear readers – actively engaging with it in relation to your own experiences and context that it comes alive. So, here are a few questions we'd like to invite you to be with before you read on. Perhaps you'd like to take them with you on a walk, to meditate on them, to do some journaling around them, to have a chat about them with someone, or to engage with them in yet an entirely different manner.

- Why is it that you, personally, feel attracted to regenerative education, or to regenerative thinking more broadly? Can you sense a link to your own biography, or to certain existential questions or feelings that you have carried with you throughout your life so far? Or can you perhaps even sense that you're in the process of taking a new step in your own thinking in or relating to the world?
- As you begin reading this book, what's your initial or current motivation to make a difference in your education context? Are there particular things in your own practice or in the community and system you're part of that strike you as undesirable, maybe even absurd? Or is there a particular potential you sense that you want to help manifest?
- Building on your reflections around the two questions above, how do you want to engage with this book? We'd like to invite you to write your reflection down in one word or a short sentence that you can hold as you continue reading.

2 Learning with a Sense of Belonging

Introducing the Story

Koen: The story I'd love to introduce here zooms in on the whole process of how we supervise higher education students towards the end of their education journeys, when they start doing graduation projects. More specifically, it relates to a group of six 2nd-year master's students in Sustainable Development at Utrecht University, with whom I engaged in a co-creative graduation experiment in the academic year 2022–2023 as part of a larger project called the Academy of Hope[1]. The core motivation driving this experiment was a shared motivation – of myself and these students – to avoid that their graduation year would feel like a productive yet superficial rat race, a journey of 'ticking the boxes' that lacked a deeper experience of purpose, connection, and relevance. A process, to refer back to my opening statement, that does little to evoke a deep sense of belonging. So, what does it mean for me as a teacher to create a setting in which to engage with students differently, to collaboratively turn the graduation year into a regenerative experience? That's what this story is about, about trying to create that community of students who co-creatively take on their graduation year – and the master's thesis as its focus point – as an opportunity to actively bring their own evolving biographies into conversation with the world. To show up, so to speak, to be touched and to touch.

Koen: So Bas, Mieke, and Sofia[2], does this provide you with enough context to do an imaging exercise?

Mieke: I've got enough; let's go!

Textbox: A Practice of Imaging

Imaging is the capacity to evoke a dynamic, alive image of an unfolding event, situation, or process. Imaging is a whole-body experience of tuning into the essence of something. It comes close to the regenerative notion of 'seeing potential', and is different from *imagining*, which relies on fantasy. There are multiple entry points into an imaging mind, or way of seeing, some which might resonate with you more naturally than others. In our own experience, imaging generates added value to a regenerative thinking process when practised both consciously and consistently. Different settings may require different entry points into imaging, for instance, when in conversation with a colleague or student you may not feel the space to close your eyes to see more clearly, yet rather develop your capacity to bring alive an image of what they are working on through asking conscious questions. In other instances, such as we developed together in this chapter, a way to do imaging can involve an embodied practice, which brings in the whole of the body-mind, or the wisdom we carry as human beings beyond just our brains.

We ourselves have been taught to practise the difference between imagination and imaging through reflecting on swimming - something that almost all Dutch people would have an active relationship to. First, as you read this, can you intuitively come up with a few terms that describe what swimming means to you? Note these down. Now, after reading this sentence, we invite you to briefly close your eyes and *swim*. After you have opened your eyes again, what did you notice about this last experience? For Bas, for example, this exercise brought back a lively image and bodily experience he had in the Arctic Circle in the summer of 2023, when he swam in Odin's Bay. The exercise for him conjures up the increasingly rare feelings of painlessness that frigid waters cause, and the awe of the rolling mountains as they jut up from the bay.

In the following chapters, our imaging practice sometimes results in almost metaphorical images, and sometimes rather concrete pictures of what something/someone could be(come). These imagings then become a rich basis from which to enliven thinking from a more embodied, conscious place in the conversations that follow. In order to bring alive this practice of imaging, we invite you to take a break yourself once you get to the parts in the text where we were closing our eyes for a moment, and consider doing the same yourself.

Imaging the story

Bas: Is it okay if I go first? Yeah, so actually, my imaging started while you were still introducing your story, Koen, and it was so powerful that I couldn't really stop it. I had this image of a woman looking at a mirror, and in that mirror was the globe. And it felt super violent in a way, in the sense that we ask students to do projects geared at healing the globe, but they themselves remain unseen. Like, we don't ask them to engage in a process of mutual healing with the world. It's more about: Can you do something that adds to my research agenda? Or something like that. This now seems to me a very extractive, forceful, violent relationship, and this came to the surface for me very strongly. Yet what also emerged was that same person being in a different relationship with that mirror. By also seeing, and painting on, themselves. In a way, I started seeing a transformation of worldly engagement. It shifted from this initial kind of instrumental thinking towards an engagement of figuring out your own narrative or your biography in and with the world. And, accordingly, the role that you can take, as an educator, to facilitate that different relationship for your students. This came up for me almost instantly and didn't let me go. A process of mirroring with and in the world, with the intention of helping students figure out what their place in it could be, instead of asking them to engage with the world to extract something from them. I don't know necessarily if I would call this shift hopeful, but it holds the potential for it to be, I think. And it's also not a move back to a sort of student-centred individualism. Yes, it is about acknowledging the individual, but it's about that person's relationship with the whole. That's what came up for me.

Sofia: In my imaging, I saw more like that whole you mentioned at the end, Bas. I didn't so much focus on one student, but more on the intention with the community of students to go through a shared journey together. I saw a big, single sunflower that then turned into a field of sunflowers. The sunflowers, symbolizing the group of students, looked kind of the same, but then there was also a lot of biodiversity amongst them. And there was the sun, shining on them, and the flowers turning towards it. And it felt like there was lots of diversity in how each sunflower related to the sun. The sun, I think, symbolises knowledge, and its light is both common to and uniquely experienced by each sunflower.

Mieke: Okay, so I started drawing my imaging and I also had a song that came up for me which I'd like to play first.

[Mieke plays 'Caminando', by Rising Appalachia.]

Mieke: So, just like Bas I also already started seeing a first image while you were still talking, Koen. I resisted it because I felt like 'Ah this is too esoteric, too much yoga'. So, it was literally an image of a body of light, like seeing the whole body and seeing the different layers of potential within humans, which goes beyond their intellect, and beyond head, heart, hands. The energetic body. This image of a connected and whole body symbolised a student. With it came this sense that every human being has the potential to evolve and develop as this whole, connected being, increasingly so connected to their teachers, who need to be that body of light themselves in order for that development to be invited and nourished. So that was the first part of the imaging. And then the second part, that's where that song also came up strongly, which almost feels like a life motto to me at the moment. It resonates so much with regenerative work, and every time I listen to it, I hear something new. So, the image that started forming next is one of a bunch of students and their teacher grouped together on a hiking trail through a valley, with wide mountains all around and the sun on the horizon. At some point in the song, they sing 'caminando hombro a hombro', so 'walking shoulder to shoulder', as in this image. So as a teacher, becoming a regenerative educator is really to see the whole potential of the human being that you have the privilege and honour to work with and to walk alongside *'hacia el sol'*, towards the sun.

Koen: Beautiful, thanks for all your imaging. The image that came up for me strongly resonates with all those that you shared. So, I started having this image of students sitting in a hot tub together and myself, as a teacher, sitting amongst them.

There's this comfort, the comfort of slowing down and just sitting in that nice, warm water. Sort of connected by the flowing water. Then, like a flash, I thought 'Is it ethical to sit in a hot tub with students?' but I managed to postpone judgement and go along with the image. Then the image started evolving. So, whereas first it was an image of connection and comfort and slowing down, I started seeing that there are several things that are being reflected by the water as you sit there together. So, you see your own reflection as you look down into the water, as if the water is posing the question of who you are. But then at the same time, you see clouds, and birds, and mountaintops or whatnot all around; you see the world reflected in the water. Just like that mirror in Bas's imaging. So, as you're sitting in this comfortable hot tub, you sort of face this reflection of self-in-world, posed as a question. And then the image started shifting again, and, in their own time, people in the hot tub started getting up with determination, in a way that communicates that it's the exact right time to get up and they know just what they've got to do in the world. Encouraged by the knowledge that there's always this hot tub to get back into, to be resourced and to be called by the sun – to speak with both Sofia's and Mieke's image – to get up and go on an adventure once more.

Bas: In listening to all this imaging, there's a memory that suddenly popped up for me. Some time ago, during a hike in Norway, someone told me: 'It looks like you're a part of the landscape here'. This touched me deeply. The reason it comes up for me now, I think, is that it resonates strongly with the way we're imaging regenerative education in this conversation. That is, as a journey that's geared toward this experience of truly belonging within the landscape of where you are.

Koen: I find that beautifully put, Bas. It's about encouraging and nurturing students to do the work that somehow belongs to them and makes them belong.

A Deep Dive into the Story

Koen: So, I'll try to develop the story in some more detail now. In early 2022, when I had just entered the faculty of geosciences at Utrecht University as a postdoctoral researcher, I started relating to the master's programs that were being taught there. And I started observing a few things in connection to each other. One was that I noticed that the students I spoke with, being in the faculty they were in, were really concerned about the planetary crisis. And they seemed to me quite ready and eager to contribute to sustainability transitions. I also sensed that some of them were feeling a bit lost in the education system, experiencing anxiety, stress, and a need to slow down and take better care of themselves. Looking at the last year of the program, I realised that the thesis projects they have to do are really big projects. They're 45 ECTS[3] projects, that's three quarters of the year's study load. I read through the course guide of the master's thesis and found it so old school: impersonal and strongly positivistic in approach, not really inviting more participatory research approaches.

So, I started thinking about how I could initiate an experiment to do things differently. That's how the idea for a thesis community emerged. Together with a few colleagues, I came up with 'the post-fossil good life' as an overarching thesis theme – that is to say: What does it mean and ask of us to live meaningful lives in a way that moves beyond extractivist cultures and systems? Then I basically just sent out an open invitation to students asking them if they'd like to be part of a thesis community rather than it being an individual project, and if they'd like to really get the space to shape their own projects within, and supported by, this community. Within this broad umbrella of the post-fossil good life, I asked them: How are you touched by what's going on in the world and what is the way in which you feel a need or a desire to respond or to touch the world back in return? Then we had a group of students who said, 'Yes, I want to do that!' and we basically collaboratively created the programme as the year progressed. It was a very interesting and inspiring journey, which I can say many different things about, but I think the thing that I want to emphasize here and now is that I realised that it really takes a lot of patience, courage, and what I like to call 'loving resistance' to create the conditions for students to really dare to live that question I posed them: 'How am I touched and what is my way to respond?'

For many reasons, it's so easy to walk away from that question because it's scary or we're too busy and so forth. I'm reminded now of one particular student – but I could tell a similar story about any of the other students – who came in with this very clear story about 'care work'. She said, 'So there's this need in the circular society that we're moving towards to really appreciate the often invisible work that's done in the background to create the conditions for such a society to thrive.' Things like repair work – think of mending clothes and the maintenance and repair of technological tools – and how we process waste in increasingly circular ways until it's no longer waste at all. She really wanted to do something about re-appreciating, re-thinking the kind of care work that's crucial in light of circular economies and the emancipation this would entail for certain historically undervalued workforces. Then slowly, while I was supervising her, she tended to shift away in directions related to this initial motivation, but – in my perception – lacking important elements of it as well. For instance, there was this relatively easy opportunity she spotted of connecting to initiatives and research around installing solar panels on roofs. Yet this was much more about establishing a new workforce than about emancipating an existing one, and about installing as many new technologies as possible rather than about repairing or re-using materials. Eventually, she ended up doing half a year of participatory ethnography in a 'recycling street' in Utrecht, in which she became a worker on the recycling street and collected data drawn from her own experiences and interactions with her co-workers. Interpreting her data through a care lens, which she developed herself, she lay bare elements of the embodied knowledge of her co-workers and offered critical perspectives on how recycling workers can be empowered in the context of a circular economy. Although it was a challenging process for her, in which she became disappointed or discouraged along the way on several occasions, she felt like she had done something that she deeply cared about, brought her closer to herself, and offered a meaningful contribution to society. My observation was that her work was appreciated by the people she interacted with, and when I spoke to her last, at her graduation, she told me she'd found a job at the municipality in which she would work exactly on the themes of her thesis. She'd managed to make her graduation year *her* graduation year. I felt deeply fulfilled by seeing this happen. And, although it was truly her accomplishment, I also had to think back to the resistance I had offered her along the way. On several occasions, she had seen an easier or clearer path – e.g. the installing solar panels route. On those occasions, I would typically provide resistance and ask, 'Is this really what you should be doing?' and then she would be like, 'Shit, do you have to ask that question?' And then the next time we spoke, she'd be like, 'Yeah, yeah, yeah, this was actually not what I really have to do'. My task was to really be supportive of her journey, but also to gently hold her accountable for its direction. I mean, it's easy to say to students that you want to give them space to do what they feel they really should be doing, but to then actually facilitate that process in a way in which potentiality actually comes to fruition is a whole different thing. It was an interesting experience, different in relation to every individual student.

Bas: So, it sounds a little bit, to me at least, like staying with the trouble. You know, like Donna Haraway's work[4]. You said, 'It's very easy to walk away to take the easier path instead of the regenerative path'. I'm very curious what it's like for you as a teacher in those situations to navigate or to cultivate ... facilitate... to nurture someone, to actually stay with that trouble. Like, how is that for you?

Koen: I keep asking myself the questions 'What agenda am I pursuing here? What interests am I trying to serve?' There are a few directions in which I can easily be pulled, and if I allow that to happen, I'm not going to be able to help students in this way anymore. One of the forces that can pull me away are my own interests. For instance, I might have reason to really want to focus on solar panels. And then think, 'Oh, yes, this student is now going towards solar panels. Great! Let me jump on this train and make it happen'. Or I might think about what is going to be a trajectory for me to have this process with this student be a relatively easy one, in which we straight-forwardly match the criteria of the programme and can 'tick all the boxes' without too much hassle. These are things that I consciously have to resist; instead, I am to practice really listening to the potential of who this student is becoming or trying to become in relationship to their context. I am to pose the question: What wants to emerge here? I sense that if I really dare to do that, I intuitively tend to feel like, 'Wait a minute, this is a moment where I need to slow down and resist'. This is not something that is very rational! But in order to feel and act on that intuition, you need to have this sort of peace of mind and the presence, yourself, to really focus on that sensing ... that's the big challenge. Really being present, rather than having an agenda beforehand that needs to be fulfilled in this or that way[5].

Mieke: What is resourcing you then, in your role as an educator, as a supervisor, to be able to show up as present and available and tuned in, as you describe? How do you do that? How do you become a resource to your students?

Koen: I think I really invest a lot of energy in relationship building. So, for instance, the first thing I did with each individual student who wanted to participate in this experiment, was to take them on a 1 to 2 hour walk in the botanical gardens of our university and get to know each other. I'd openly share why I'm doing this, what my concerns are, what I care about, and most of all I'd ask questions about their unfolding stories and listen. From those initial conversations and then, of course, in dialogues that followed afterwards, I started developing quite a feeling for who these students are and what their process is, which makes it something you can fall back on. Of course, those considerations are hypothetical because I can be wrong in my judgements. And I never said to these students something like 'No, this is a wrong direction, you should do this instead'. So, there is definitely something here about staying humble about my input to students, about asking them questions and openly sharing observations, rather than instructing them what to do. But all in all, this relationship building provided quite a good compass for my intuition. Besides that, I really noticed in myself that my ability to do this work rapidly decreases once I'm stressed or have a lot of other things on my plate. What I usually try to do is to plan 1-on-1 meetings with students around 10:00 a.m. and to spend the morning till then to prepare. This way, I'd only think about other work tasks afterwards, so that I could really be tuned in to that particular student.

Bas: That's really interesting. I just have to think about some of my own past experiences now of having to assess four or five bachelor's theses a day for days on end. I've had times when I had barely looked at a bachelor thesis, and then found myself saying things like 'It's really interesting that you highlight this or that', without really feeling what I was saying. So, yeah, I think that there is a need to create certain conditions that are conducive to this attentive approach. I mean, don't you struggle to uphold this quality of your work with students in the existing institutional context?

Koen: Of course I do, and it is actually in part because of this that I wanted to shape this experiment as a communal thing. I'll take this as an opportunity to say a bit more about that. So, we had a group of six students, and I came together with them throughout the whole year quite intensively. In the first part of the year, it was every two weeks, then we had a phase in which it was every week, and then when they were deeper into their thesis research, it became every three weeks. The students would do a bunch of stuff together without my presence as well, and we really co-created what we did together when we all met: Exploring the overarching story that the theses tell together and expressing it creatively. Reading and discussing literature together. Holding methodological discussions and workshops, for instance about doing ethnographic research or about dealing with issues of positionality. Students hosting workshops for each other, to address themes they'd encountered in their projects together. At some point we started dedicating meeting time for students to actively resource each other's thesis work. Of course, they also did fun things together, and I probably only know half of it. Going for drinks or organizing potlucks, all these kinds of things emerged. Having this community element, and sharing responsibility for it, made it a lot easier to uphold the quality of how we were trying to work with each other, and it made the whole journey a lot richer than if it had only been me trying to supervise a single student in a different way. This also enriched my relationship with them, because in those communal moments, I could really take on a different role than when I was supervising a single student, and I could really see that the students were getting inspiration or support not just from me but from each other. Which, in fact, made everything much more doable for me! Sharing the responsibility of resourcing each other is what made this different approach to graduating doable. It created a lot of space for me to actually step back and trust the process. I may have initiated it, but to a large extent, the students created this community aspect. And it was, as they told me, what attracted them perhaps even the most in embarking on this collective journey.

Mieke: Your story brings up a question for me which I have been reflecting on as well, on what this tells us about the principles or the groundwork of co-creation processes, about what is needed for meaningful co-creation, and for co-creative mutual learning communities to emerge.

Koen: I spoke already about relationship building with individual students, but I reckon you're inviting me to speak a bit more about community building, beyond my individual relationship with students. Maybe it's interesting to sketch a small scene of one particular session we had. So, at some point, we invited a small group of practitioners who were also interested in that question of the post-fossil good life to join our students for several sessions of collaborative inquiry. These practitioners held positions related to sustainability research, sustainable financing, teaching, regenerative farming, and personal leadership training. More importantly, they were puzzled by similar questions as the group of students. So, we basically said, 'Hey, we have six students working on these themes, we have a few practitioners interested in them, let's see what happens if we bring them together over a period of time'. You know, a very emergent process. In that process, my role was to facilitate collective inquiry. So, in preparation for the first session, I asked them to do a few things. I asked them to audio-record a story of an experience in their lives that to them feels somewhat like 'a seed of the future', an experience that really signals what it might mean to live in harmony with each other and nature. I also asked them to bring some source of inspiration, which could be a book or it could be an art piece or it could be whatever they wanted, as long as it really inspired them. Lastly, I asked them to write a text of about 250 worlds that communicated their deepest desire for our collective future. So, prior to the meeting, I decorated the meeting room with all these works. I created a sort of mini-museum. The future dreams were displayed on a few windows. There were some couches in a corner, where I put a few laptops with headphones on which the audio-recorded stories played in a loop. And there was a large table on which the sources of inspiration were displayed. So, after a welcome and getting to know each other a bit, I told them we were gathered in 'the museum of our collective consciousness', and I simply invited them to visit it for an hour or so. They could interact with each other, and with the materials displayed in the museum, at their own pace.

That's how we started the learning process for this group. Rather than starting with theory or a guest lecture or whatnot, I tried to communicate: 'It's the worldly experiences, dreams, and questions that linger in our collective consciousness that form the heart of our curriculum, so let's get to know each other intimately'. I think it was starting by creating this sort of sacred space, this museum of our collective consciousness, that awakened the potential for this group to start experiencing that they, first of all, are a group and, second of all, have a collective regenerative potential. I feel that creating that space to connect with each other on this biographical and existential level is really important.

Mieke: I mean, as a student, that must feel so much like being seen and being valued. I wonder for you as an educator, what resource do you draw from in caring so much for the potential of that community to design this kind of session, to hold that space?

Koen: Going back to my opening statement to this book, I personally really experienced a lack of intimacy in the education system. That lack of intimacy is exactly the opposite of what I'm trying to do here. Like, when I was a student, from primary school through to university, was I truly heard? Was I sufficiently invited or supported to be 'touched' by others, by the world? Was I encouraged to meet the world in a sincere attempt to look the big questions of today in the eye? For me, in my experience, the answer to all these questions was more often no than yes. Yet I really needed that space, because I was just from a young age onwards struggling to find meaning and connection in a world that to me seemed so harsh and troubled in terms of how we're working and living together, and in terms of the values that we prioritize. So, I just was always looking for ways to belong in the world, and I felt like school was not supporting that search. And that became my focus, my main interest, in the last phase of my time as a university student and the first years of my career as an educator and researcher. Like, why is this happening? What is this all about? And the tentative answer I came to has a lot to do with that we've forgotten how important relationships are[6]. That we've forgotten that in the end education isn't, or shouldn't be, first and foremost about acquiring a set of skills and knowledges, but about practicing to relate to oneself, each other, the world in ways that are meaningful and appropriate and from which the development of potential can occur.

So, what are good relationships? What are proper relationships in education settings? What are meaningful relationships in a world that in many ways is in crisis? For me, a very important part of the answer is to create that radical space for taking up individual and collective biographies, and to see the potential in them. That's where the real connection comes from and where the potential for initiatives that come from a position of love can emerge. A loving engagement with your own biography. To me that's a crucial part of taking responsibility for our collective, shared world. So, yeah, creating radical space for it in education is, for me, a very intentional act.

Mieke: Is this then for you also a quest for or an exploration of how you become more at home in the education system and, connected to that, how that experience is for those that you work with, like students and colleagues? So, about your relationship with the system?

Koen: I feel that for me to be at home in the education system or, more specifically, in the university or department that I'm in, is to be able to create space for these more relational, intimate ways of working and learning together. And I find this quite hard. So, the university department this story is situated in is full of staff and students who really want to make a positive impact in society regarding climate change. With the students participating in this experiment, we at some point developed a metaphor of the bodybuilder. So, it's this idea of really pumping yourself up as much as you can in order to save the world, to do good, and through doing so, actually breaking your own body.

Bas: Very unrelatable [said in a jocular tone].

Koen: For some students this was a really powerful metaphor, to start seeing 'Oh, wait, I don't have to become this perfect person who is some sort of hero. It's enough to ask the question "From everything that's going on, what really touches me, and what is my way to respond constructively through my evolving life story?"' This allowed it to become so much more relatable, doable, and hopeful. It was really about slowing down and creating space in order to move with purpose and determination. I feel that creating this kind of space is what I've got to offer within contemporary education systems. This story has been particularly about doing that together with students, but I find myself increasingly focusing on how to do these things with colleagues as well, and how to actively try to open doors for spreading this type of work throughout education systems. So, I am quite looking forward to the two chapters we'll co-create next, which will zoom in exactly on these dimensions!

Reflective Questions

The reflective questions we offer here and after each of the chapters that follow are grounded in regenerative concepts and premises and emerge directly from the text you just read. We invite you to find (and experiment with) your own way of working with these questions, for instance by creating a moment for journaling or reflective writing or by going for a walk. In our experience, these questions can come further to life when they are (also) explored in conversation with another person. While we encourage you to briefly explore and reflect on each of the questions below, you might find that some of these questions especially resonate with you in this moment and choose to spend a bit more time with those.

- How can I truly co-create learning processes with students and foster a sense of community and mutual support and learning?
- How can I contribute to healthier relationships and relationship building in my (formal or non-formal) education context?

- How can I truly see and value the regenerative potential of the people and systems I work with?
- Where in my education context can I sense potential for regenerative experimentation, and how and with whom can I take initiative?
- How can I nurture a (learning) space where people can explore what really touches them?
- How can I nurture a (learning) space where people can experience a sense of vocation?
- How can I create and nourish a healthy balance or resonance between self-care and taking responsibility for or in the world, both for myself and for the people I work with?
- How can I open up education processes for active involvement of and engagement with place, community, and practitioners?
- How can I hold myself and those around me accountable for the direction and potential of learning processes?

Invitation to Disrupt Educational Relationships

Dear reader,

In the story I've been exploring in this chapter together with Mieke, Bas, and Sofia, I've spoken of my habit to start working with students by going on a walk together. I've also shared details of a 'museum of our collective consciousness' teaching method that I've played around with. I wanted to take this opportunity to devote a few more words to the potential of orchestrating education interactions and relationships in such ways, and to encourage you to (continue to) play around with this yourself. We're so accustomed in contemporary education systems to engage with each other *indoors*, *seated*, and *transactionally*. By and large, that's the setting in which students and teachers interact with each other. I find that when I want to shift gears to do more holistic, co-creative, and potential-oriented work with students, it helps to place myself and my students in a very different setting, with other rules or invitations for how to engage with each other. I've come to experience this as a rather playful and fun dimension of my work. Overall, I sense my students and colleagues feel the same. More often than not, my 'victims' experience it as refreshing and vitalizing to be dragged out of business-as-usual modes of interaction. And I certainly experience it that way myself.

Indeed, something changes when you walk side by side with students through nature. It's wondrous to see how conversations become more personal, more natural, and more open. Time and again I have observed how nature helps regulate conversations as well. Taking a break at an open field with a nice view invites something else than walking through a dense section of a forest. Whenever I invite students or colleagues on a walk, I do so with a general intention in mind, but I also purposefully try to leave space for the conversation to develop as it wants to. I find that appropriate to do; I almost feel like nature demands it.

Something changes, also, when you purposefully redesign a classroom, as in the case of 'the museum of our collective consciousness'. More and more, I find myself getting rid of tables, and often even chairs. I want my students to be able to move around, to fill the classroom with objects or materials that they've brought or prepared, and to engage with each other in dynamic and developmental ways. And I'm increasingly aware that if that's what I'm aiming for, I need to co-create environments that accommodate and invite it.

So, I guess the final questions I want to close this chapter with are these: What kind of interactional patterns are you aspiring to in your relationship with your students and colleagues? And how could you disrupt 'business as usual' to create settings and spaces that accommodate and invite that kind of interaction?

With love,
Koen

Notes

1. Together with one of these students, Koen also published a paper about this experiment. Wessels, K.R., & Grünwald, L. (2023). Fulfilling the regenerative potential of higher education: A collaborative auto-ethnography. *Education Sciences, 13*, 1037. DOI 10.3390/educsci13101037.
2. Sofia participated in the setting up of the conversations that formed the basis for this and the next two chapters of the book, as part of her student assistantship. She joined our collective imaging process as well.
3. In the European Credits Transfer and Accumulation System, each credit corresponds to roughly 28 hours of study, so a total of 1260 hours are dedicated to the graduation project in their final master's year. Note that the amount of time dedicated to graduation theses and projects varies quite drastically across different master's programmes in Europe (and likely beyond).
4. Haraway, D.J. (2016). *Staying with the trouble: Making kin in the Chthulocene*. Duke University Press. While the work is a quite complex philosophical treatise, its major theme is the interconnectedness of beings and the question of how to take responsibility for your own actions amidst the messiness this implies.
5. See Bastiaansen, E. (2021). *Aandachtige betrokkenheid als pedagogische grondhouding / Attentive involvement as pedagogical disposition*. Universiteit voor Humanistiek. See also the fifth chapter of Koen's PhD, about the practice of being present in the moment and acting with integrity. Wessels, K. R. (2022). *Pedagogy of entanglement: A response to the complex societal challenges that permeate our lives*. Utrecht University Repository.
6. An important source of inspiration for me (Koen), in this regard, has been Hartmut Rosa's (2019, 2020) critique of modernity. In short, Rosa explores how we've come to depend on an economy and culture of acceleration, growth, and possession rather than on qualitatively rich experiences – experiences of resonance, as he puts it. Rosa, H. (2019). *Resonance: A sociology of our relationship to the world*. Polity Press; (2020) *The uncontrollability of the world*. Polity Press.

3 Guerrilla Gardening and Resourcing

Introducing the Story

Mieke: Our next story is about the FRIS community, which is a community within the University of Amsterdam working on education innovation for a fair, resilient, and inclusive society. So, fair, resilient societies – the F, R, and S – stand for one of the four thematic priority areas of the university's strategic institutional plan until 2026. For each of these four strategic themes, the university's Teaching and Learning Centre, in collaboration with the Institute for Interdisciplinary Studies, organizes and finances thematic teaching innovation scholarship rounds. My involvement in FRIS started with an invitation from different people who knew me directly or had heard of me, and they saw me taking up a role in coordinating and supervising this round of scholarships and creating a learning community connected to it. I said yes to the invitation, not knowing exactly what it involved, but somehow sensing the potential of co-creating a space and community within our institute focused on innovation, and the possibility of bringing more regenerative-inspired ways of learning and working.

At home, they often joke about how for each new project I embark on, I somehow come up with another acronym. When I was invited to work on the FRS theme, together with a colleague who also acts as our university's chief diversity officer, we felt the need to connect the fair and resilient narrative to a more inclusive discourse, and hence we came up with the idea of adding the *I* of *inclusive* and, *voilà*, the acronym FRIS was born. *Fris* means 'fresh' in Dutch, which, interestingly, has really become a way in which members have come to characterize the community we started to form, and our shared community identity.

To paint a somewhat more colourful picture of what the FRIS community has evolved into, let me share a few more details on how this scholarship programme has evolved slowly into a more regenerative place for educators who are interested in innovation and who care about connecting education to the theme of fair, resilient, and inclusive societies. At the moment of this conversation, the call for teaching innovation proposals was first opened a year and a half ago, and there have been three rounds of grant applications so far, in which we selected about 20 projects with about 30 grantees.[1] Together with two colleagues employed by the Teaching and Learning Centre and, a bit later on, a student assistant, we've worked on creating a learning community of education innovators, through organizing a series of developmental workshops, called FRIS cafés. There's a core group of people who come very consistently to these bi-monthly FRIS cafés, and these people have also been at the basis of co-creating the name and what it would look like.[2] So, there's that enthusiasm and commitment. There's also a bigger community that is interested, but often cannot create the time and space to make it to sessions – which are perhaps illustrations of the overheated system we characterised in the introduction. During the initial phase, there was a clear wish from the community to first establish a closed, safe space and inner community, only for grantees. Now, after a year and a half, the community has developed a collective desire, and perhaps courage, to open up our events to other educators and colleagues.

So, I think the value of the FRIS story lies in exploring what happens if you intentionally co-create a learning community within the university for educators coming from very different parts of the institute and bringing a wide diversity of habitual teaching practices, as well as varied aspirations for innovation. And what happens when you allow people to pause and reflect on the deeper purpose and aims of their innovation aspirations, through regenerative framework thinking and contemplative pedagogies? So, before we resume our practice of imaging, let me share a quote from one of the grantees who is in the faculty of business and said during one of the FRIS cafés: 'This is such a different space to be in; it's the only place in the university where I am invited to develop myself as an educator. Perhaps we should add a subtitle to the term FRIS cafés and call these sessions regenerative retreats for teachers'.

Koen: It's starting to come alive.

Bas: Yeah, let's move on to imaging; I'm just very curious what will come up.

Imaging the Story

[We kindly invite you to join us in imaging this story.]

Koen: Partially triggered by the name, I started imaging something refreshing. So, I started seeing this image of a small fountain. And this brought me back to a very hot day in Sevilla, Spain, about twelve years ago. It was over 40 degrees Celsius, and I walked into a park with a woman I'd just met – the same woman, in fact, that I mentioned in my opening statement. In the middle of that park, we found a beautiful fountain, and we ran right into it, allowing it to refresh us. Around us, others were doing the exact same thing. This fountain, as I remember it, was a place for refreshment, but also one where people connected with each other and experienced intimacy and inspiration, although this was probably partially the butterflies talking. The fountain was a resource, with people coming in and out, regenerating them in those hot Andalusian summer days. And then the image started to evolve, and I started seeing, like, a swarm of bees buzzing around the fountain, sort of in between the fountain and whatever the people in the fountain had going on in the world. To me, it felt like this symbolised all the academic buzz, chit-chat, and cognitive overload that we know all too well. I mean, even in the acronym FRIS, there's already four big words, right, which we can debate endlessly, as we love doing in the academic world, and there are strategic themes and all kinds of arrangements and funds and whatnot. Like, it's so easy to, metaphorically, become dehydrated, to become disconnected from the connection, freshness, and inspiration of the fountain. So, yeah, I guess that's my image of the FRIS community. A fountain providing refreshment, connection, and inspiration, and a flow of water from that fountain to the day-to-day work of its community members, resisting the omnipresent and often overwhelming buzz of academia.

Bas: I had an image of people sitting around a campfire toasting marshmallows. You know, chill vibes, someone playing some country music, which – sidenote – I love, with a guitar, cooking over the fire together. And then, the way you were describing it made me think of the first time someone didn't just eat marshmallows on a stick but decided to make s'mores – which is this genius combination of toasted marshmallow and chocolate sandwiched between two biscuits – and that really stuck with me. Like, what happens if you bring together different things? Turns out: delicious food. But I'm sure they also tried other stuff that was not great. They must've taken a few times to figure out that it was chocolate and crackers, like maybe they tried something like Oreos and concluded it wasn't quite it. It feels to me like FRIS is this kind of communal, co-creative, 'campfire-like' space as well, where there is room for brave experimentation which is allowed to also fail, within safe boundaries.

Sofia: Thanks. I like the sweetness of the campfire and the melted chocolate a lot. Getting quite hungry now in fact... And, yeah, also the connection, the sense of community of the campfire and the intimacy in the fountain. In my imaging, I was wondering what the story by Mieke is bringing us. And in doing so, my imaging went more into your direction, Mieke. Like, I could imagine you growing up with this FRIS community. So, I guess I was wondering how this educator-to-educator space holds a story of a communitarian growing together, and support between each other, or also struggles perhaps with colleagues...

Mieke: Thanks, Sofia. Can you say more about the direction of the potential that you could see or feel?

Sofia: It's about you engaging with that community of other educators and – amidst these personal connections and intimacies – building up a way to regenerate education.

Mieke: Thank you. That's really cool. It's so much more interesting when you're crafting an image together this way, and there's quite some resonance with what I imaged myself. So, what came up for me was the visual of guerilla gardening. Like, in cities, where you just lift up paving tiles and you green up the space without necessarily asking permission or approval. It actually reminds me of how a few parents connected to the school community where our kids belong to suggested we not wait for the municipality to green up the schoolgrounds of our new school building, but we just start to lift up a few tiles ourselves. It connects a bit to what you and I spoke about earlier in a podcast episode, Bas[3], about the university being this concrete stone, very urbanised, dry, not so fertile or nourishing space. I imaged that what the FRIS community has the potential to grow into is this sort of cheeky guerrilla gardening movement. Where we connect to our environments with freshness and new energy. Where we get to travel through the different faculties spread across the city and weave them together. And to really invest and care about how we are going to meet, the energy and vibe in the rooms, the catering, you know, the design of being together, with full presence.

So, for me, this idea of guerrilla gardening is connected to seeing the potential of a place and bringing more aliveness and play and joy. I also connected to what you tapped into, Sofia; I could also see myself in that inner-development phase, growing together and evolving together with colleagues. And weaving who we are becoming as more FRIS-inspired educators into what outer developments and meta-crises are calling us to become.[4] And realizing that I didn't know what I was saying yes to when I got the invitation, but that this was one of those invitations that if they come your way, you know deep inside that you're going to have to say yes, even though you tell yourself you're taking time to carefully consider all types of constraints.

Recently, a colleague said to me, 'Oh, but the FRIS community won't last forever, right? I mean, it'll be another half a year or so, and then you'll probably just let it go.' And while the comment was made in a informal setting, I experienced it as quite confrontational, and somewhat uncomfortable to hear. I didn't immediately know what to do with it, really. So that was interesting; the colleague reminded me of a natural bureaucratic restraining force we often encounter in education institutes, of budget cycles determining the life-course of projects, sometimes even changing financial commitments because of changing priorities and strategies. My discomfort with realizing that the end of this community might arise sooner than expected or hoped for illustrates something about my caring about and commitment to it. It also opens up a more reconciliatory perspective, where the inevitable end of project funding – or in some cases the initial absence of such funding – does not have to mean there is not enough hydrogen to fuel the vitality and evolution of the project, and that viability does not only consist of money.

Just like with a campfire, if you stop putting wood on the fire, it's going to extinguish. And there is so much busy-ness in the university pulling you back and forth, a bit like the swarm of bees Koen saw. A day-to-day busy-ness which numbs you to feeling alive, away from the fountain, away from the campfire, and falling back towards numbness and mechanicalness in the way we repeat what we've done before as educators from an efficiency and automatic mode of behaviour at the level of existence that Sanford talks about[5]. As a community, like the name implies, FRIS is really meant to be an invitation to become more awake against such mechanical forces. And to re-source yourself as an educator with fresh inspiration, solidarity, and encouragement to continue on your education journey.

Deep Dive into the Story

Koen: I guess we have quite a lively image now. Yeah, of a group of people within the university as an urbanised environment full of stones. You're coming together, you're a bit playful, maybe a bit naughty, a bit sneaky here and there. And you're just, like, taking out stones and letting whatever is under there grow again. So that's quite a clear image. I feel like we're probably going to go towards your role within this and what it means for you to play that role. But maybe we can start with you giving us a livelier sense of why this came into being and what was sort of crucial in that process of enlivening?

Mieke: The emergence of FRIS started with this coalescence of different people's visions and commitment to revalue education and revitalize the quality of academic teaching from an interdisciplinary and thematic perspective, and then inviting me to lead this project. My prior projects led to that point, as these gave me the space to experiment and play with regeneratively designed education, and slowly build some stories around that. One of those projects was the Critical Development and Diversity Explorations, which gave some visibility to me as an innovative educator, and to some of the regenerative ways of working. Even though the regenerative elements of that were initially implicit, later connecting it to my research and writing about it created more visibility. There was also a project called STORIE, which we developed with a team of colleagues and societal partners for a Comenius senior grant proposal[6], which connected regenerative thinking with approaches to inclusive education through storytelling. Unfortunately, we did not win that grant-lottery ticket, which felt like a disappointment regarding the collective energy and love we had put into these plans with an amazing group of colleagues and societal stakeholders. However, together with one co-applicant, I decided, 'Okay, we didn't get the funding, but we're still going to bring this work into being in an adapted, pilot version'. Luckily, we then managed to negotiate some support from the chief diversity office, which gave both of us a bit of time to experiment with a pilot, which we then called CREATE.[7]

With the CREATE pilot, we set out to bring together a group of motivated students and teachers, educators, and support staff, to work together on reconnecting to everyone's intrinsic motivation and will with regards to their role in the university ecosystem. And doing so from a regenerative place and design. We had a group of about thirteen people joining us for that journey. It was great and challenging and a lot of fun, even as we managed to play between on-site and online settings during the COVID-19 lockdowns. After that first pilot, we explored opportunities to further develop a co-creative, cross-hierarchical learning community like CREATE to land somewhere in our institute, and at that moment the FRIS initiative emerged, and that invitation made its way to me.

Koen: It's really interesting to see the nature of the process. So, I'm triggered to think about the characteristics of a process that leads to regenerative collaborations within education systems. Listening to the story you just told, I think there are some characteristics that highlighted themselves. For one, the process was very emergent. You just started doing all kinds of things without getting the funding or the long-term strategies or plans, but doing it anyway. And then somehow one thing led to another. You went for grants, but you didn't get them. At least initially. But then later you were recognised for the work and you actually got the invitation. What do you take from this?

Mieke: I mean, for me, if it wasn't for the work I've been doing with the regenerative development community and the Regenesis Institute, a global network of regenerative thinkers and doers[8], I feel like I would not have been able to do all that kind of exploratory, adventurous work, not knowing where it was going and investing a lot of time and energy in projects that are very irregular in an academic career[9]. These entanglements give me a constant invitation, but also a healthy discipline to clarify my own direction and my own purpose – my long-thought question. It is about seeing the bigger picture of doing all these very niche, small-scale interventions and observing where in the system there might be space. And it's about trying to somehow create more space to allow this energy that we saw in the image of the joy and the campfire and the refreshing fountain to flow within a university. I gained trust in the belief that regenerative ways of working, and being within the university ecosystem was actually possible, because of my experiences of working with students and innovation projects. What if we would create a space for more teachers that have a desire to reconnect to their love and passion for becoming a regenerative educator? One that does not just follow the machinery of the system, but is seeking alternative, kinder, more meaningful and loving paths for learning within academia? So, I guess it's really clarifying my own pole star and having this pole star to guide my navigation within and beyond the so-called education system.

Having a clear pole star to direct my energy was likely also why I knew I would say yes when the invitation for the FRIS community came, even though the invitation wasn't that clear and the regenerative approach wasn't part of that initial opening. I actually felt a lot of restraining forces with regard to the 'resilience' part of the invitation, which is something I wrote about in an academic blog, critiquing the whole move towards resilience as a concept in the humanitarian field. So, if I would have just stayed within the academic buzz and the concepts and put on my critical academic hat. I might have said 'no'. And if I had listened to well-intended career advice pointing to more regular career choices, I should have said no. But because I could stay in touch with the bigger picture of the potential I can see in the system to lift up some tiles and start community guerilla gardening projects, I could enter into it with trust. Trust is key. Trust and courage, daring to do things differently and having the trust that even if things do not go exactly as we hoped, like with the grants, it is not thrown-away energy, it's an investment in potential. It didn't fail; it just turned out differently. Those steps became stepping stones to something we couldn't imagine yet. It reminds me a bit of when one of the community members said, 'Oh! This is not going to last forever, right?' and I felt very protective of this growing guerrilla garden we are nurturing. What if I don't want it to die? Maybe it's not necessarily up to us to keep that particular garden growing, but to transport the seeds from this garden to others, so that we may nourish the broader education system.

Bas: I find it super interesting that, in a highly ironic way, you're almost working on your own resilience to be able to keep engaging with the temporality of the gardening act you just described. Not responding reactively from protectiveness but seeing it as a part in a creative process. It sounds like a very healthy way of engaging with the sort of irregular, naughty, and adventurous academic guerrilla gardening you're describing, but I'm very curious how that resonates with you.

Mieke: Yeah, that feeling sounds like what we experienced with the FRIS community café meetings. You know, it's very good and well to create safe and cozy communities of people who want to do things differently. And the social connection that comes with that helps to make you feel very happy together, in a sort of self-congratulatory way. Patting each other on the back about how it is going and how innovative we are, and not feeling alone in that. There is definitely power in that, but it doesn't lead to system transformation by itself. You need an appropriate amount of discomfort, self-accountability, and ability to open up and connect with restraining forces with those who don't naturally gravitate to something like a FRIS Café. It's this navigational act, where you are continuously dancing between systems, translating, navigating. It would be very interesting to explore the research in urban studies on guerrilla gardening and what actually happens in 'real' guerrilla gardens! I'm also thinking in relation to your question that my first thought went to who can actually step up and co-hold these types of spaces, especially when there are restraining forces. And it asks from myself the ability to be less protective, to let go of something like the FRIS community if it expands and shared leadership is redistributed. Trusting the community to guide the co-evolution of FRIS instead of it just depending on my guidance.

Koen: So maybe you can say a bit more about this? You've said quite some things about the work you need(ed) to do inside yourself to show up in these spaces in ways that are nurturing. What about the way you work together with others in these contexts? What are, in your experience, the core dynamics across the different communities and projects?

Mieke: Thanks, Koen, that's a helpful question. It's quite interesting to notice that in the FRIS community, I'm actively working on how I need to show up in this space in terms of how I can hold the space and facilitate connections and a deeper introspective reflection. To not remain at the surface, where we only cognitively engage, but to really feel and connect with joy, discomfort, and the rest of the spectrum wheel of emotions and experiences we normally filter out of academic life.

And it's not just me carrying that within the community. Interestingly enough, quite a few of my colleagues in the FRIS community have also, in their co-creation roles, offered contemplative practices or deeper inquiry perspectives. It's really a place for me where I'm figuring out how to lead a community from a regenerative perspective, to step up when needed and step back and create space for others to flourish. Where I work more as a resource, holding a space like a fountain or a campfire where people come to light their torches or fill their water bottles. That type of energy can't just come from me, and at the same time, it's not just holding space. There is also a need to be an educator with a vision, and someone who creates the conditions for further collective envisioning. And it requires from me to continuously evolve myself in the field of regenerative development, to stay just a little bit ahead of where my colleagues are, when we are journeying together. *Caminando*, shoulder to shoulder.

Koen: It sounds to me like what you're inviting us into is somewhat of a move towards resourceful educator-to-educator relationships. Where educators can support each other in their regenerative journeys. Where they aren't in a state of competition with each other, or holding each other back. Where we don't benchmark each other in a controlling way, but nurture and challenge each other to develop.

Mieke: Yes, that resonates. So, I started with the regenerative work in the reiki community. In the reiki community there are five precepts that are a core element of the spiritual practice. One of the precepts is to honour your parents, teachers, and elders. I try to connect with this through remembering the respect and responsibility for seven generations into the past and into possible futures and I find it really powerful in the context of bringing in a regenerative perspective when you're co-creating education. This perspective allows me to ask questions which place present day education design choices in relation to the longer histories that played into this current moment, and the future aspirations which lie ahead. It also allows me to reflect on my own role as educator, and how and when you need to step back in order for co-creation to happen and others to step up, while at the same time recognizing that that there is an active role to play as a teacher or as an educator involved in community-based learning and development. And that's also the value that I see in a community like FRIS, where, as educators, you can almost reconnect to that sense of the deep responsibility that you carry working with students and colleagues. The future generations that we care for and whom we aspire to support in their development towards maturity in the world. But to be able to be there for each other, it is important as educators to recognise and invest in communities and mentors that function as your fountain, your resource. And to invest in and commit to building a sense of togetherness that is often absent in the system, for students and educators alike.

That also aligns with what you are saying, Koen. The sort of competitive, teacher-of-the-year-award teacher, who has the highest evaluations, and who can publish a ridiculous number of academic texts, and so on. The competitiveness is also reproduced in how we work with our students, with the grading and assessment systems. So, yeah, I guess it is about trying to explore how to create or nurture developmental learning communities that live out regenerative principles. I'm thinking of the mycelium we talked about when we just walked in the forest before recording this conversation, and all of the mushrooms that sprouted from this invisible connective network below the ground. The type of learning ecosystems we aim for are like how trees and fungi and forests thrive. When I transpose that to the academic system, I mostly see the opposite. I see it in the teachers who are supposedly weaker or who always take too much time to grade the exams and are therefore scolded by the exam committees and receive negative reviews and complaints from the students. What happens currently is that those teachers get pushed out or that the system tries to remould them, often through scolding. Anything, really, to get them to fit into the efficiency model. Maybe there's some care and support from other teachers, but how much time do you actually have to truly do that? Where do you take the time to help and support and nourish when you have your own courseload to worry about? That's not how trees, fungi, or mycelium work. Within their intricate systems, they care for each other and co-evolve, like when one tree will communicate to others that there are harmful microbes or when certain trees need more hydration and they exchange water or nutrients through the underground mycelium[10].

I wonder what it would mean if we saw teachers as one of the trees that make up the forest of the university. And for whatever reason a particular tree is struggling that may actually be a great restraining force for the forest as a whole. You know, maybe one teacher taking more time to grade is actually a wonderful thing. They may be truly taking the time and care needed to attend to this task with the proper time that the task requires. Perhaps those 'trees' should be applauded instead.

Bas: There is something I find really quite beautiful in the perspective shift you just proposed. When a teacher, or several teachers, are not reaching the set-out goals or are not aligning with what's being requested, currently the tendency is to look at this as an individual problem. Like, 'Oh, it's Dr. Harris again'. They are not good enough, or fast enough, or whatever enough. In a way, your proposal shifts this to see these 'unhealthy' trees as symptoms of an unhealthy forest instead of the cause. And as restraining forces to be welcomed as part of the entire situation. That shift alone can have a transformational impact on how you look at and engage with education systems.

Koen: Connected to this shift to accountability on a system level, it's really encouraging to see, as you described it, that others are stepping into the FRIS community with the intention of being co-owners of the space. Stepping in to offer gifts like contemplative practices for the benefit of the whole community.

Mieke: Yes, well, of course we do invite them to actively co-create.

Koen: It's one thing to hand out the invitation to take that type of co-ownership but something else entirely to hold the energy with which that invitation is truly felt. There is something magical about that, right? Magical in the sense that it may be fleeting and rare moments where you feel like there is this togetherness. Where everyone is participating in a way that simultaneously makes them teachers and learners. Like everyone is giving part of who they are to the whole of community and there is a shared responsibility to make things work. One person may offer to bring lunch or snacks, and someone else may intuit that an energizer is needed and bring that in. But what is needed to get to that point, where the members of the community feel okay in stepping forward to the whole? Where you shift away from individual competitiveness to seeing and nurturing the forest?

Mieke: So, one of the first FRIS participants attended a recent FRIS Café, and there were only about 10 members or so of the larger community (of about 50) at this session. And the first thing he said was, 'People do not know what they are missing; we need to make sure that people come here! This is so valuable. This is the only place where I get to work on myself as an educator. Where I feel like I love my job again.' While it was interesting to hear his positivity about the process, it also really affected the energy of the room, and I felt a need to step in as resource. Basically, in that moment, I decided to change the plan I had made beforehand to start the session with sharing and working with a particular framework. Instead, I proposed to do a tailor-made wake up exercise first, so that we could bring everyone along in their own kind of thinking and trajectory into this community.

It was an interesting play of 'Okay, thank you. This is really beautiful and let's pause, let's contain that energy and let everyone first connect to themselves and their own will and motivation, and then from that collective energy explore further'. And when we did that, we actually had some opposing voices come into the conversation, which was really beautiful to see. And that particular colleague could still bring in his perspective, but now there were also other voices that brought in something different. Which is a part of creating learning cultures that are aspiring to be more inclusive. It's about creating spaces where you can connect to your own experience and inner work and share them, connecting to the outside and community and the system in respectful manners. That's fundamentally different from debating, which happens all the time in academia. You know, where the strongest argument or opinion wins the debate.

Bas: Or the loudest voice.

Mieke: Or the loudest voice, which is oftentimes a male voice.

Koen: Two questions in response… So, firstly, could you give words to your own role in this situation? And secondly, you've been talking quite a bit about being a resource for others, but what is resourcing you in these situations?

Mieke: [Talking in a jocular tone and feeling increasingly hot] So, you mean: Can I try to come up with a definition of what it means to become a regenerative educator? Ah, that's such an easy question, ha-ha. So, yeah.... It definitely has to do with staying connected to that pole star I spoke about earlier in this conversation. What is the bigger systemic change or the whole that we as a community care about collectively? How can I hold that within me in the role that I was invited to play, and that I choose to play in this community from a place of external considerations and deep caring for the potential of each member in the community? How can I cherish both loud and soft voices and both spoken and unspoken words? The resourcing I need to do is layered. It has to do with daring to be courageous enough to be your whole self in the multiple roles that you hold, and commit to a continuous, lifelong learning and development process yourself, so you can show up with increasing levels of consciousness and skill. For me, that means a daily discipline of working on my state of energy and being. Concretely, I start each day with my spiritual practices of reiki and yoga. This grounds me and enables me to remember during the day to show up as a regenerative partner, a regenerative parent, a regenerative family member, a regenerative educator. The embodied and spiritual practice I commit to daily, as well as the communities I am part of, like Regenesis and the Dutch-based reiki resource community, allow me to stay committed to my own development in showing up in regenerative ways.[11]

Koen: Can I share one observation? It's really striking how, within a few sentences, you mentioned that you had a plan to work with a specific framework in this session but then decided not to do that because something else was needed. So, you let go of a plan and followed the flow. Yet as you did this, you halted the particular, strong voice and energy that motivated you to change plans in the first place. So, there is this duality of being very flexible and willing to let go of your plans but also, on the other hand, this mindful stubbornness to make sure we're evolving in a regenerative track. You don't mind deviating from plans, but only if that deviation puts you more on track.

Bas: That balancing act was also very clear to me when you were talking about the person saying FRIS may be ending soon. It was very clear to me that there was some tension in a way in that moment.

Mieke: Can you say more?

Bas: Well, on the one hand you highlight that FRIS may evolve in unanticipated ways or disappear altogether and that you're not fully in control of all that, nor can you always fully understand the deeper, long-term meaning of such things. Thus, you try to be super-open and flexible. But then at the same time, you have the other side of the coin of feeling very protective when someone proposes that something that you care about, like FRIS, may end, and mustering up the resilience to make sure its potential isn't just squandered away within the bureaucracy and politics of the university.

Koen: But the holy grail here that tells you when to be flexible and when to be stubborn. That is, as you were saying...

Mieke: ...holding a pole star in mind. And in order to be able to see the pole star, you need to tap into the water of the fountain so that the buzz and the rush and the noise... and the cloud of smoke from the campfire isn't obscuring the clarity of vision of this star in the night sky.

Koen: You're clearly doing that yourself as a daily practice. But it also seems like you are taking the responsibility of creating and protecting the space for everyone to connect to that pole star, in their own ways.

Mieke: Yeah, and to find their own pole star. And see if there's a shared image – like a constellation of stars – that we can remember to look at as we navigate the waters of life and the land of education systems.

Bas: There's a very radical act that you mentioned as an aside there. You didn't press the pause button in that FRIS meeting to silence or disrupt a dialogue, you pressed it to invite more diversity into the space. I think there is a fundamental radicalism to that. Which is qualitatively different from the more standard academic manager or leader type, who would often use those types of interventions to bypass or overrule voices. It felt quite radical but in a soft and gentle way. It reminds me a bit of Judo in a way. As you know, I did Judo for a very long time and even studied its philosophical underpinnings quite extensively, which – fun fact – emerged mostly from John Dewey's work[12]. But Judo literally means 'the gentle way'[13], moving with and leveraging forces and movements to transform their direction. Perhaps you are a gentle radical, Mieke.

Mieke: For me, the Law of Three is helpful here because it allows me to look at what is unfolding and find a third path, which opens the way for a new level of understanding or state to evolve. The Law of Three is a framework I got to know through the Regenesis Institute and the work of Carol Sanford, and it proposes a trio of forces that are always at play: activating, restraining, and reconciling forces. It is visualised as three arrows, two pointing to the centre and one – the reconciling third force – moving up from that centre (see figure 2). The first of these looks at what forces are trying to change, affirm, or bring something into activation; the second looks at what is trying to conserve, receive, or restrain; the third, the reconciling force, attempts to bring them together and transcend them (see the invitation to reconcile after this chapter). All three forces are always present in events or situations, yet it takes practice and courage to be able to recognise, and embrace, all three of them.

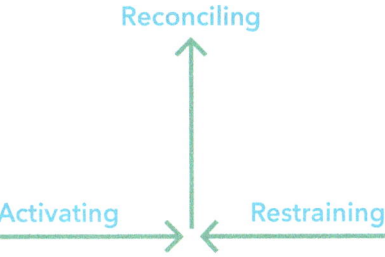

Figure 2: The Law of Three (Bennett, 1993:36).[14]

In this case there was a very strong activating force. It was really powerful and energizing, but the Law of Three allowed me to move with what emerged in the moment and pause, to create space for other voices – and thus more restraining forces – to also be heard. The restraining force can sometimes also function as a receptive force, where it contains the energy. Not getting stuck between activating and restraining forces, but connecting to the potential of a reconciling force, in this case, was done by inviting people to (re)connect with their own pole star – and together explore a possible shared sense of direction which we hadn't thought of before. It resulted in a co-created design of a FRIS festival, where a much broader audience was invited into a larger learning space. Bringing in the diverse and opposing voices within the community, in the end, allowed us to lift ourselves up to a new level of discernment and thinking and creativity and caring. What often happens if you follow only one strong voice, whoever shouts the loudest leads the way, which is usually what happens in academia.

Bas: Yeah, that's what I meant, the stance or attitude that you bring into these types of spaces is radical compared to that loud-voice mentality that reigns supreme in education contexts. A radical softness *and* mindful stubbornness.

Mieke: It feels like finding the courage, together, to see the potential places for guerilla gardening in our education contexts and then caring for and resourcing the growth of developmental learning communities.

Reflective Questions

Similar to the former reflective questions invitation, we encourage you to now create some time and space to engage with these questions in a way that works for you at this moment.

- How can I design learning spaces in such a way that they work with consciousness of the histories (as far as seven generations back) of the people and places they are embedded in, and take responsibility for future (seven) generations ahead?
- How can I co-create and manifest the regenerative potential that I see in people, places, and groups around me, and in doing so, bring together different departments, disciplines, and peoples?

- How do I exemplify purposefully slowing down in education spaces, and bring the cooling energy of water to the overheated education system around me?
- How can I nurture my courage to step up in the spirit of guerilla gardening and experiment with planting the seeds for radically new ways of learning, and support others in doing the same?
- How can I stay with the discomfort that can occur in this work?
- How can I nourish spaces where discomfort is welcomed?
- How can I hold on to the learning communities/places that I breathe life into lightly enough that I can also let them go when they no longer serve the bigger potential?
- How can I become more aware of and work with the activating, restraining, and potential reconciling forces (from the Law of Three framework) at play in challenging situations in my work or life?
- How can I develop my capabilities to image the potential of what could become manifested, and in doing so gain clarity of the pole star image I use to navigate and make choices for more regenerative educatorship?

Invitation to be with the Law of Three

Dear reader,

As you've seen in this chapter, I aim to practice *being* a resource for the people I have the honour to work with. This means, among other things, to really be present in the moment and to tune in to what framework might be useful in that situation. Because my work is placed in the current polarised and inequitable fields of the university, the broader education system, and even society today, the Law of Three framework is often useful. Hence, I try to hold this framework alive in my mind – and my being – when I'm leading or facilitating sessions or events, such as a FRIS Café. I wanted to take this opportunity to say a bit more about how I practice to bring alive this framework, and how it enables me to co-create communities and processes that are more developmental in nature. Perhaps this framework can help you, too, to become increasingly aware of the dynamics in your teams, and to (continue to) develop your ability to sense and work towards potential, while working from all there is.

In the world of education, and specifically in academia, we are so accustomed to thinking in terms of defining problems, understanding them, and then solving them. Something I see happening quite often is that, consequently, there is a sense of polarisation appearing – of stuckness, of conflict, and of 'no way out', sometimes in myself, sometimes in teams, sometimes in an institute or in society at large. For me, these are useful signals to wake myself up and remember that looking through the lens of a Law of Three might allow me – and others – to see things differently. To elevate the quality and consciousness of our thinking, and explore truly new, radically different perspectives. And to snap us out of automatic patterns of thinking and behaving – and open up to seeing new potential.

Similar to other dynamic living system frameworks we work with in this book, the Law of Three is not a conceptual model or traditional academic framework that you can just intellectually 'get'. Instead, after working with this framework for about a decade now, I've experienced that it's a framework that becomes meaningful when you are able to really *be* it. It took me a few years, really, for this framework to become alive and present within my awareness enough that I can remember it when I encounter a situation – bigger or small – which could benefit from it. To get there, I started by practicing to purposefully bring it into the design of situations, events, conversations, and community gatherings. From there on, I slowly started noticing more intuitively if and when this framework could be appropriate to elevate the quality of interactions and work. Yet even after working with this framework for years, it's easy for me to slip back into an automatic mind. That's why I continue to seek regular resourcing support from 'friends in the work', which is crucial for my own ongoing development of showing up as usefully, present, and meaningfully as I can. Each time again.

Perhaps you can bring to mind a recent challenging situation in your life. One that felt tense in the moment, perhaps when there was a conflict or misunderstanding. Maybe a quarrel with someone you love, a difference in views with a colleague, or a tense moment in a learning setting. Potentially, looking through the Law or Three can allow you to sense and see more clearly a missed opportunity for something more meaningful to have happened. Start from lightly connecting to the whole of these three interconnected forces, and invite a sense of openness to really explore – in an unattached manner – the added value of each force in this situation. Connecting to the activating forces, what happens in how you cultivate a sense of sincere caring about what's going on in the situation? What happens if you open up to how restraining forces might be welcomed or seen as meaningful – yet often challenging – parts of a whole picture. Or turn your thinking a bit upside down, and see these forces as receptive or containing, instead of restraining? Notice, then, what happens in your thinking and state of being when you turn to explore the reconciling forces which might not have been visible before. Similar to what I wrote above, it is truly helpful and perhaps necessary to invite a resource to support you in doing this work.

Making a first step, or even commitment, to learn to *be* with the Law of Three is something I have experienced as a courage-requiring step to take. To step out of stuckness or complaints and to creatively explore what potential there is for a regenerative move. I hope to meet you somewhere in this movement and walk together.

With love,
Mieke

Notes

1. For more info on the FRIS community and the innovation projects included, see the webpage https://tlc.uva.nl/en/article/sig-fair-resilient-inclusive-societies-fris/
2. For more details, see Lopes Cardozo, M.T.A. and Petersen, S.P. (2024), Regenerative guide for co-creating education innovation communities - the story of FRIS: Fair, Resilient and Inclusive Societies at the University of Amsterdam, University of Amsterdam's Teaching and Learning Centre and Institute for Interdisciplinary Studies. Link: https://tlc.uva.nl/wp-content/uploads/2024/10/Regenerative-Guide-FRIS-Final-oct.-2024.pdf
3. Please also see 'The University as a Constructive Disruptor', a Podcast conversation between Mieke and Bas at The Regeneration Lab, available on all major podcasting platforms. Link: https://podcastaddict.com/the-regeneration-lab/episode/137388139
4. Inspired by the work of Shaukat Lupson, N. (2023). *What is the metacrises?* podcast series Entangled World, https://najialupson.substack.com/about
5. See the introduction, where we introduced the Levels of Work Framework.
6. This is one of the subsidy grants for education innovation in The Netherlands. STORIE stands for Supporting the Transformation of our Organisation by Regenerating Inclusive Education.
7. CREATE was the name given to a "winter-to-spring training on academic-civic engagement & inspiration" in which we aimed "to regenerate ourselves, serving our communities in and beyond this university", which ran between January and May 2022 and included students, phds, support staff and research/teaching staff.
8. See https://regenesisgroup.com and https://www.regenerat.es
9. Referring here to how, generally speaking, academics are primarily 'judged' in terms of funding obtained in prestigious research grant schemes and on output in the form of peer-reviewed journal articles. Any activities that don't directly lead to more of those could be considered irregular career moves.
10. See, for example, Sheldrake, M. (2021). *Entangled life: How fungi make our worlds, change our minds and shape our futures.* Vintage Publishers.
11. Mieke also reflected on this unfolding experience of exploring what it means to *walk the talk* of becoming a regenerative educator in this article: Lopes Cardozo, M. T. A. (2023). Walking the talk: Autoethnographic reflections on co-creating regenerative education within international development studies. *Third World Quarterly, 44*(7), 1625-1642. DOI 10.1080/01436597.2023.2197206
12. John Dewey wrote widely on progressive forms of education. His writings on art experience (1934), nature (1925), and democracy (1915) influenced Dr. Kano in his work on Judo as a developmental system.
13. As part of his doctoral research, Bas conducted an autoethnographic

engagement with regenerative education, which he catalogued as a series of *Medium* articles. One of these zoomed in on his previous experiences with the philosophy and practice of teaching Judo, before he lost this ability due to disability and illness. See also this *Medium* article that he wrote about Judo and regeneration: Van den Berg, B. (2020). Towards regenerative learning ecologies – Teachings from Judo. *Medium*, 31 December. https://medium.com/mission-impact/towards-regenerative-learning-ecologies-teachings-from-judo-5982731c15a0.

14   The Law of Three framework was initially coined by the Armenian philosopher George Gurdjieff (1877–1949) in the 1920s during his teachings (Seamon 2020). One of his students, John G. Bennett (1897–1974), integrated the wisdom received from Gurdjieff and Peter Ouspensky (1878–1947) as his philosophical and spiritual teachers into his own work as a mathematician and philosopher. He developed an approach called *Elementary Systematics* (Bennet 1993). The framework has since been adopted and re-developed by Pamela Mang, Ben Haggard, and colleagues at the Regenesis Group in Santa Fe, New Mexico, into a larger technology/methodology referred to as regenerative design and development (Mang & Haggard, 2016; Hes & du Plessis, 2015, pp. 123–124). More details about how this can be applied in thinking about education systems are given by Lopes Cardozo (2022). Bennet, J. B. (1993). In D. Seamon (Ed.), *Elementary Systematics – A Tool for Understanding Wholes*. Based on the original manuscript from 1963, Bennett Books, Santa Fe, New Mexico; Mang, P., & Haggard, B. (2016). *Regenerative Development: A Framework for Evolving Sustainability*. Santa Fe: Regenesis; Hes, D. and Du Plessis, C. (2015). *Designing for hope: Pathways to regenerative sustainability.* Routledge; Lopes Cardozo, M. T. A. (2022). Learning to become smart radicals: A regenerative lens on the potential for peace and reconciliation through youth and education systems. *Journal on Education in Emergencies, 8*(1), 187-213. DOI 10.33682/3qpc-3v3y

4 Hospicing and Acupuncture

Introducing the Story

Bas: Having spent two chapters exploring this from the perspective of educator–student and educator–educator relationships, I now want to share some experiences that allow us to explore what it means to relate regeneratively to the 'architecture' of education – the rules, systems, and organising principles that our institutes bring to life. So, I'll be zooming in primarily on my own university – The Hague University of Applied Sciences – but also, more broadly, on some forces from outside, like the Dutch ministry of education. As a general introduction, I'd like to share that I often feel like my work takes place in a sort of liminal space of doing the education work that is demanded by the current system and nurturing the potentiality of what may be possible. I believe it is in this liminal space that I can develop a regenerative relationship to contemporary education systems, neither accepting business as usual as an unchangeable reality nor deserting it altogether. Often, at least so has been my experience, this begins with moments of running into restraining forces of some kind, those moments when 'the system says no' – for instance, and I'll share more about this example in a bit, exam regulations not allowing team-based interdisciplinary graduations working on real-world challenges[1]. Or, at least, there being a perception amongst actors involved – teachers, students, managers, directors, but also computers and software – that this is not a valid option. My initial, automatic response to encountering such restraining forces is to go, like, 'Right, let's try to break that down by running straight at it!' Yet this is not always the most regenerative option. I mean, I'm sure I'll run into more doors in the future, but I feel like I'm learning to nurture in myself the kindness and grace needed to do so in ways that provide space for others. Showing up regeneratively, in this sense, involves truly accepting that there may be obstacles *and* acknowledging that from the perspective of different system logics, these obstacles may even (have) perform(ed) very important ecosystem functions – although often these are outdated logics that are no longer fit for purpose. But it's also about trying to find ways to navigate around these obstacles, to work in the shadows, the nooks and crannies, under the radar. And about engaging with this work with patience and (very) long time horizons. It may be impossible to graduate as a group of students now, but a new policy plan cycle is coming in three… four… five or however many years[2]. So, what seeds may I plant now that may flourish by then? It may be the case that you end up planting seeds that you never get to see blossom. These are some of the core themes I would like to explore more deeply in this chapter….

Koen: It feels like what it gives us in terms of imaging is you as a person trying to engage with restraining systemic forces in a regenerative way, trying to figure out what that means and building the capacity to do so.

Mieke: Is there something more to contextualise? What is the system you are navigating with(in)?

Bas: Yeah, so, I'll expand a bit on when we tried to facilitate collaborative graduation. The intention of that intervention was to allow students to co-create a single artifact (e.g. like a thesis, film, podcast, design, play, etc.) that they can use as the basis for their collective graduation requirements, allowing multiple students to graduate in an inter- or even transdisciplinary project using a singular expression of learning. Or in more regular speech, 'a single learning product'. What we did to explore this idea was, first, go on an internal expedition within the university, where we involved a broad set of actors, literally all the way from the executive board to students and pretty much anything you can imagine in terms of managers, teachers, researchers, and professors in between. What happened was, at the time, both frustrating and fascinating. We encountered this sort of dichotomy where there was broad support when we spoke with all of them individually, but when we tried to actually implement it, move it from a potential to a reality, we encountered collective resistance. 'Well, but that's not allowed because of exam regulations' or 'The computer systems cannot do that' or 'If they do inter- or transdisciplinary work, we won't know if they will be "proper" engineers or social workers or teachers' or 'Graduation is supposed to be individual' – and restraining forces like those. No one was very clear if they were talking about norms, policies, regulations, or just plain old belief when they made these arguments, which I found interesting as a scholar. Ironically, when I examined the actual documents from the university and the ministry of education, I didn't find anything that explicitly stated that graduation as a team is impossible or undesirable. There was nothing, at least in terms of written policy or regulations, holding the idea back from manifesting in the world. It was just a living norm that was seen as an infallible truth in a self-perpetuating system. The moment when you start trying to roll out an idea or intervention, like graduating as a group, more systemically, these types of restraining forces tend to show up strongly, quickly, and fiercely. Part of the guerilla gardening work – to refer to the previous chapter – in those situations is to explore what space to do things differently you actually have. What is the capacity of the system you are entangled with for the potential that you see to be manifested? That may mean you have to accept that you will not achieve what you were aiming for right now. But are there steps you can still take, seeds that can still be planted?

So, I think this inspired my reflections: experiencing individuals saying yes, but then when you try to move towards systemic level work, as a whole, those yeses turning into nos. The other moment I want to highlight took place quite recently, actually, when I worked with our ministry of education to do a video and photo interview, essentially just discussing my PhD as part of a series they do on education change makers. I must admit this was done during a very contemptuous time in our national politics – the elections were a few days later – and once the video and texts came online, two of our national parties took bits and pieces out of the video and text to make quite angry political content and tried to use that to attack the ministry and myself personally on social media. The ministry decided to take it down and contacted me about what was going on and said they had to reconvene internally to consider if they could republish it and in what way. They said part of the reason they took it down was previous experience with quite nasty online bullying for previous speakers who were talking about 'contentious' topics. While I appreciated them looking out for me, it also raised some fundamental questions about freedom of academic speech and, I'd say, also the responsibility the ministry has to present topics that may be confrontational.[3] That was quite a tension to be with.

Imaging the Story

[We kindly invite you to join us imaging this story]

Mieke: That was quite emotional imaging for me. What I saw was you, but in the role of a regenerative education leader. Sort of like you were stepping into the arena with the courage to step up. And it almost was like a kind of a bullfight, which is a very not regenerative image. But there was this kind of energy, running at that goal, running at that red cloth and just people watching and the vulnerability of what that emerged into. So, that was kind of like, whoa, this is harsh and painful. And then it softened, and it became more like a theatre setting... but still held a quality of stepping up. And then I had kind of the real image of you sitting on stage with the recent book that you launched[4], where you were in the launch panel and what it takes to step up and be there. Then I was transported to our walk just now in the woods. Where we encountered a big tree that had fallen over the path and you kind of literally said, 'Oh, well, there's an obstacle. So, we could run into it, but we could also find a path around it.' The physical act of us four trying to find a path around this tree, slipping and sliding in the mud as we did so, having to slow down, it really takes more time, it requires slowing down. It's a collective act of caring, of reaching out a hand to make sure that everyone is okay. This resulted in a switch in the imaging away from pictures towards a question. What is the overarching story that wanted to be told in relation to these three moments? And then I just felt quite a lot of pain and sadness. There's a lot of restraining force, and its hard work to step into that space.

Sofia: I also had similar images that didn't feel very regenerative at first, but I was, like, 'Okay, wait a second. It's okay. All this discomfort with these images I'm seeing is... just okay; let's go through the uncomfortableness.' In the first one, I saw a mountain peak that was dark with a lot of crows and other flying animals around there. And I was, like, 'Oh, what a mountain!' Then in the second one, I saw a boat that was surrounded by this circular movement of sharks. Then in the third one, I saw a theatre with actors on stage with these fake, masquerade faces, symbolising the hypocrisy present in our institutes. I wasn't able to clearly see real faces. A common theme I sensed across all three images relates to the process of dying as part of the emergence of new life. A bit like in the fall, when there are a lot of leaves on the ground; dying needs to accompany regeneration. So, the topic of dying, of letting go, of grieving and daring to connect with discomfort and pain, was very present for me. And I tried to just be with that.

Koen: I had a clear image within the first two seconds of the exercise, and then I spent the rest of the time unpacking it. So, you know how these big trash bins tend to have very large lids? And how, if you put something inside and put the lid on, it it's gone, binned away, no longer your problem? What I saw was you in that bin, trying to climb out of it, and someone or something else trying to close the lid on you. A bit like having a door thrown in your face. That felt very harsh! But then I thought, the lid is not just pressing you down, but it's also protecting you from the dangers 'out there', like all those systemic forces that want to restrain you, that can crush your initiatives, exist behind that lid. The lid allows you to see them, in a protected way. So, you can pause and try to calmly peek around the edges of the lid and figure out strategies that may be more successful in changing the system. Like the moment we see the tree blocking the road, it's like, 'Oh, okay, that's the obstacle. But now I can pause and explore possible ways to deal with this obstacle.' So, I had this double sense of, 'Oh, this is painful, being pushed down like that' and, on the other hand, 'Hey, this is enabling me to actually make this happen, because now that I see what the forces are, I can start to understand the system, and I can figure out what the right questions are to ask and what the right responses are to actually make meaningful change through working with these forces'. Until the moment that the lid is being put down on you, you can't see those restraining forces clearly. You're basically just guessing what and where they are. What does it mean to have this double relationship to these restraining forces?

Deep Dive into the Story

Mieke: We need the restraining forces.

Koen: Yeah, in a way, we need restraining forces to be able to see possible pathways that we may tread.

Bas: The need and power of restraining forces is definitely something that I have been thinking and being with a lot lately. Mieke, you raised the question of what the common thread across these three experiences that I shared might be. I think actually it has to do with stepping up. To not only go to the edges of what the system can handle right now, but to stand on those edges, endure having the lid being closed on you, and to still choose to peek around and embrace that this is where the real regenerative work starts. For me, it's this liminal space between system-ableness and its potential-beyond-ableness where the regenerative educators or regenerative leader's work becomes meaningful, difficult, and, indeed, potentially painful.

Sofia, your imaging related strongly to something I've been thinking about a lot lately. Namely, that this regenerative work in the liminal space has a sort of double nature. On the one hand it's all about finding places where you can change the architecture of the education system, about finding what has been described as the system's acupuncture points[5], or places where there may be some space for movement with the right amount of pressure. So that something new can come into being. But I increasingly experience that it is in equal amount about hospicing about caringly supporting decay and letting go. This, indeed, is work that emerges from a deep position of caring. Whether that may be in the examples I mentioned or the myriads of others I'm sure you can think of. For me, engaging with that work of systemic acupuncture and hospicing feels like taking responsibility for what the world is asking from me.

Koen: These ideas are fascinating me, Bas! I would love you to expand a bit on both these notions of systemic acupuncture and hospicing. Could you give us a livelier sense of what that looks like in practice, perhaps through one or multiple of the stories you started sharing?

Bas: When I mentioned hospicing in this setting, I mean something that is quite analogous to hospicing in the medical setting. It's something that really takes a lot of development as a person, but what I mean is that you learn to see existing system configurations as something that people tie a lot of their identity, love, and care into. In a way, the systems as they are become unconscious or conscious extensions of who they are becoming. And trying to help to change that is like letting go of something that is alive and loved but that may not be entirely appropriate anymore. For me, for example, being diagnosed with ankylosing spondylitis meant I was no longer able to engage in the sports I was committed to, necessitating a need to redefine myself. And just like a grandparent's time passes and they deserve a dignified, caring, loving exit off this plane of existence, the same type of perspective, of caring and hospicing, is needed, I believe, in education change work or regenerative leadership in education.

So, going back to the graduating-as-a-group example: When I tried to change graduation procedures at the system level, I went in with this energy of 'Well, that needs to change and let's do it like this', completely ignoring the value of what already was and the values that people assigned to the ways things were. In a way, I was conducting a potentially violent act on colleagues' identities. I wasn't considering the potential challenge my intervention posed to their professional selves at that time; I had not yet reached the maturity to be able to do that. Consequently, even though the proposed change, graduation as a group, may be a step towards more regenerative forms of education architecture, I didn't walk a regenerative path to pursue that potential for those entangled with the system as it is now. At the time, I didn't consider my intervention to be that drastic, but I now see that this was in great part because I wasn't appropriately considering or truly seeing how much a system's status quo becomes part of the people who live with(in) it. In hindsight, I would step into such a situation more gently, to explore not just how things are or why a system acts the way it does – which are still essential – but also the meaning that different actors assign to the current functioning and what it would mean for them to change. I'd aim to step into the conversation with love and care, and resolve, to be there with them through these changes.

So, this shift in perspective requires acknowledging that changing something like the way we go about graduation actually requires care and grief work. It's a process of letting go[6]. A lot of people, and people especially in education[7], derive a large part of their identity from what they do, and when you propose changes to what they are doing, you are in a way attacking them. It's a subtle but, I believe, important point to grasp if one is to move regeneratively amongst degenerative systems. Engaging with the regenerative work, stepping up, so to speak, calls for doing hospicing. Acknowledging the way things are *and* that they are not yet or not fully the way we would like them to be from a regenerative perspective. A large part of the regenerative work is holding that tension and being there with others to help them hospice or let go, so that they may become ready to engage with what is possible beyond what is.

To turn to your question about systemic acupuncture: First off, that's not a term I came up with[8]. It's based on the perspective that systems can be quite resilient and that our ability to change them in a controlled way is rather limited. Of course, we know that cognitively from systems theory[9]. But I suspect that quite a few people, including myself, still harbour aspirations to change something like education in an entire country, or perhaps even the world. But even when we draw it closer to the programs or faculties we are entangled with(in), it's not a matter of singular interventions to change the architecture of the education system. Because changing a system like education is just way too complex and interrelated. And then I am talking about the curricula, the culture, grading, and such things. Truly stepping into that limitation is painful; there are quite severe limitations to what you can achieve (in a short time horizon) in the realm of the architecture of education. Systems acupuncture provides a way to simultaneously acknowledge those limitations and still move forward. The perspective argues for the metaphor of acupuncture to say that while the entire program, institute, or country's education system is too strong a monster to tackle, there still might be weak spots that can be intervened in. There may be chinks in the armour that can be pressed. Part of the regenerative work lies in trying to identify those spaces where there is potential for system evolution and, hopefully, being able to purposively apply some pressure to them. And I think the only way to be able to actually identify those is through that act of stepping up and having that proverbial door shut in your face. It's only in the face of resistance that cracks become observable. For example, in the context of group-based graduations, on the other hand, I had to pivot drastically and ended up finding a minor programme that had not been taught for several years and that I could redevelop with several colleagues as a testing ground for the idea. Weaving and bobbing into spaces where there was more room for constructive dialogue. We haven't been able yet to truly manifest the potential of group-based graduation on an institutional level, but with this testing ground as a starting point, we did find other paths to take small steps towards it. In some faculties, it is now part of the conversation to at least experiment with something like it at the faculty level. In all this work, regeneratively moving with(in) education systems at times feels to me a bit akin to the Japanese art of Kintsugi, mending broken pottery with gold inlays to create something that is both old and new. I believe it is our job, our responsibility, in the regenerative field as actors in education systems to both try to break the porcelain where it's needed and to restore the cracks – wielding, in a sense, a club and gold brushes.

Koen: I really get a lively sense now of what it means in your experience to take on that role of hospicing and engaging with systemic acupuncture. You get the lid put down on you and you think… okay, this is when I need to find the places where I can apply pressure to support meaningful change, and this is when I need to really connect to and care with colleagues to help them let go of old beliefs/roles and open up to new potentialities. But getting the lid put down on you is quite painful, right? It hurts. You need to be there for people who offer resistance, and you need to find a place to work on radical innovation. How on Earth are you able to do that all in those moments?

Mieke: Can I add to that before you respond? Is that okay? In systems theory we often talk about leverage points, as positions from which we have power or influence. But the points on our bodies worked with in acupuncture are more than that; they are nodal points that are deeply connected to life forces and flows and energies. In other words, acupuncture points towards a whole-systems perspective and hyperconnectivity across scales. So, to add to Koen's question 'What happens when your body says no?' How do you deal with your own systemic health as part of the bigger living system you participate in, and how does the act or absence of self-care in itself have systemic workings?

Bas: Yeah, so these questions definitely trigger a range of reflections. To start, in order to do all that work we're talking about here, you need to be willing to live with that burden of actually stepping up. Of helping, caring, taking risks, peeking around the corner, and trying to find places where and positions from which you can change the architecture of the education system. To keep seeing those places where taking a leap of faith may be a way to plant the seeds for the regenerative potential of education to unfold. That's really difficult work and, indeed, often quite painful. Daniel Christian Wahl once said to me in this regard, when we were discussing the difficulties of regenerative work in a degenerative world, that this duality implies a strong ethic of caring that also extends to oneself. In that conversation, he talked about the prophecy of the Shambhala warriors, likening me to one of them, like many others in the broader regenerative movement[10]. To be able to be a warrior in the Buddhist sense described in that prophecy, it's crucial that you take care of yourself. Not just physically but as a whole being, with thoughts, emotions, pains, and struggles. Expressing that kindness to myself is not something I am particularly good at but something that I am working on becoming better at actively. And something that you amongst many other people I love actively try to help me with. They are also qualities I attempt to carry with me for my team. I think it's essential because the restraining forces are relentless and unyielding. They will take you down, burn you down, spit you out if you don't acknowledge that need for self-care. Of course, it doesn't help if you, like me, have the tendency to just see these doors and charge straight in hoping they will eventually budge. When you are walking a path through the woods, being able to see a fallen tree in a forest as a possibility to find new paths is not an easy thing to live for me. I think developing that perspective is also not something you do once and for all. It's a continuous journey, an active process, of deciding how you try to step up. And sometimes that means I may not be able to step up in ways that the moment is asking for me. Just like moving regeneratively in/through/with education systems is a continuous and co-evolving process. For example, when my arthritis pain is particularly bad, my own carrying capacity may be temporarily softened. And in all honesty, this is something I am actively seeking help with, both in the sense of mentoring as well as more therapeutic intervention[11].

What I've increasingly come to understand, along this path, is that there are definitely moments when I cannot oversee it all, or when I am not able to handle being kind to those who have just slammed a door in my face. Sometimes it's overwhelming. Koen and Mieke, both your stories helped illuminate the importance of being able to create moments of pausing that play a key role in trying to engage with the work in a regenerative way, and I think that applies to me as well. To be mindful and aware that these restraining forces are having an impact on my system, that they hurt. And at times, it's required to try and be kind to oneself and say it's okay to step out of the arena. Sometimes for an hour, a day, or longer. I've done that, literally, in meetings, where I've said 'I need to step out for a few minutes before we continue'. It can also be much longer. I've needed months where I was unable to do much work at all, and it even resulted in moments of me leaving particular teams because there was too much restraining force to handle. And it's not only being mindful, either; for me, a huge part of my ability to stay-with-the-troubles comes from my daily *earthfulness* practices[12].

In some ways, I think all this is part of why I decided to not continue in academia in a full-time capacity. My body, in a way, saying no. Noticing also, that the crazy speed of the academic system made it impossible to reserve enough time to be with the Earth. A fellow professor I once met during a retreat described their work as juggling. If she made sure that nothing stayed on her desk long enough, she could get through. That's not how I can sustainably work or live. And if that's what academia requires from me, I cannot fully participate. But taking those moments, short or long, also allows you to gauge if and how you are ready to step back into the arena. I think it's okay to do that. So, for me, part of the regenerative work is this ability to gauge when to step in and out of the arena[13] – an ability I'm definitely not great at yet in terms of finding balance, as I frequently stay in the arena too long. That's also something I'm hoping to develop in myself for those who are in 'my team', so that I may help guide them in their dialogical acts with their arenas.

I think, also, that my understanding of hospicing and systemic acupuncture is increasingly helping me to 'pick my battles', so to speak. In my experience, and that has a strong Dutch bias, we tend to be quite good at creating new things, pilots, ideas, and the like. But we also tend to forget that in order for something to be created, something else has to be destroyed or left to decay. I believe that interventions that combine these two, and that care equally about what was, what is, and what may become have more systemic depth than interventions that don't. I care about questions like: How did the system evolve to what it is now? How are different actors connected to the self-perpetuating force of this system? And I try to use this 'systemic depth' as a compass almost, as a way to decide what deserves my engagement. That is where a lot of my energy currently is going towards.

Koen: The way you're now describing your own 'carrying capacity', if that terminology makes sense, ties for me very strongly to 'dancing' with the system, rather than being at war with it or deserting it altogether.

Bas: Yeah, I think that's right. And that ability is going to be different for everyone. I think because of my life with arthritis I have a higher than average pain tolerance. Not everybody will, hopefully, have that. But I think all of us can develop the capacity to lean in and out of that arena. That may mean that sometimes, or even always, there are those who cannot, for whatever reason, step into the arena they are being called towards in that moment. Or it may be the case that there are days, weeks, or even years in your career when you are deeply leaning in, as well as longer stints when you have to lean out. Learning to honour that lived reality and learning to develop a sense of trust that if you take time out, others will fill that void just like you are filling it for those who are resting. You know, you are not alone in this – I hesitate to use the word – fight. But it's not a burden you have to carry by yourself. Right now, I am in many ways in a resting period, where I even decided to no longer work at the university full time. One of the reasons for that, beyond interests outside the campus, is to give my body a break.

Mieke: I noticed in myself that the strong emotion that I felt in the imaging is transforming in this dialogue. The sadness and the pain and frustration... some of that is softening through this process. But I'm curious to hear how that is for you, and I'm also still curious to hear what happened to you in imaging.

Bas: So, I've actually really struggled with imaging the last few months, and I think that has to do with my mental state. Dealing with depression doesn't leave that much space for imaging right now. I really experienced that a few months ago in The Hague when you were guiding us through a collective imaging exercise, Mieke. In this exercise you invited us to explore our core purpose, process, and values. And when I engaged with the quest of seeing my core purpose it was nothing but a black void. A valley in which nothing was reflected. I know rationally this isn't truth, or it's only a temporary one at best. I have been trying to find what it is that I really want to dedicate my life to. I think it's something akin to Atlas of the Heart, the work of Brené Brown[14]. This is a great book that provides an overview of the many different emotional states that are part of the human experience. I see contributing a similar overview of regenerative pedagogies to the field as something that may be my temporary purpose as I reset.

So, I think a lot of the work of regeneration is painful and involves grief, letting go, suffering. It's difficult. Yet, it is also beautiful, and meaningful, and normally purposeful. It's the type of work that makes you excited to leave your bed in the morning. It's exactly in these shadows that the potential for the light can be found, which, frankly – and I realize this is a huge privilege – is the only type of work I want to engage with. But regenerative educatorship is this continuous dance between lights and shadows. There are going to be moments when one side may feel stronger, when balance is missing, like my shadows right now[15]. And there are going to be moments when you need to step out of the arena, when it is your duty to recharge, recalibrate, and reconnect with your core. Or your pole star, so to speak. You don't always have to be on, and hopefully learn to accept that? It's okay to be wintering[16].

Perhaps more fundamentally, there's also a regenerative creative potential in truly being with both the light and the shadows. It's not an easy road to walk. There are likely going to be many trees on the path or tall mountains one must climb. But it's also an absolutely beautiful, breathtaking, awe-inspiring journey. A journey that allows you to take a role in changing the evolutionary direction of an institute, program, or even just a single course, which is already meaningful in its own right. But also a journey which allows you to fully experience the peaks and valleys of the human condition in your professional educatorship. The brightest lights and darkest shadows. While it's painful at times, that is a truly intense privilege to live.

Reflective Questions

You have landed again in a place in this book where we invite you to engage with these questions in a way that works for you at this moment in time.

- How can I ensure that I can stay in the arena of system regeneration? What needs to be developed and nourished (in me) and what resources of support can I activate?
- How can I be both adaptive and steadfast when I encounter restraints on the path?
- How can I pause to truly observe the system I am a part of and identify where I might effectively intervene to help move the system to a higher state of potential – like a systemic acupuncturist?
- Who or what needs hospicing support around me, and how can I help provide it? And what do I need to let go of myself?
- How can I be and stay sensitive to different perspectives, attachments, and needs as I try to bring about more just and viable education futures?
- How can I commit to small changes without losing touch with my pole star of more radical change?
- How can I value my body's health as part of the health of the greater whole?

Invitation to Ground and Let Go

Throughout this chapter, I've been talking about the importance of hospicing. I've come to see it as a key part of regenerative work to lovingly and gently de-attach from elements of education systems and cultures that are no longer fit for purpose, and to let go of them. This is hard work that each and every one of us has to do inside ourselves, and that we have to do together as communities. I would like to take this opportunity to say a bit more about what has proven to be essential for my own capacity to do my own hospicing and to show up with care and hospicing support for the communities of which I am part. I do so as an invitation to develop a practice of your own to support this difficult work.

Engaging with hospicing and letting go is not easy. Not for ourselves nor for the nested system we are embedded in. I often think back to a conversation I had with regenerative designer Daniel Wahl, in which he said the greatest challenge of being a regenerative practitioner is remembering to take care of yourself as you stand in service of others. It is something I also struggle with and a pattern I see frequently around me. If we are not taking care of ourselves, we cannot truly serve the unfolding of potential in the larger wholes of which we are part.

There are myriad ways to recharge, stay grounded, and let go of what's no longer serving you. My personal favourite is to do so through practicing earthfulness. This is a term developed by Arjan Berkhuyzen and Anemoon Elzinga on the Dutch island of Terschelling. Earthfulness refers to the the many practices of slowing down and reconnecting with the living world. Perhaps the easiest way to do so is to go walking in nature, and this I try to do as much as I can. I often plan a series of three daily walks in the Biesbosch nature reserve, close to my home. Whenever I have the chance, my partner and I go stargazing. That's not always easy, considering the light pollution where we live. But there is something absolutely magical about being out in the cold umbral sky and seeing our small portion of the universe. Occasionally, I get to take ice baths in the far north of Europe. It's obvious to me that these practices of earthfulness are essential to my own regeneration, but I'm increasingly aware that it also makes me more able to hospice the systems of which I'm part. It helps me to work on systems change with love, care, and support for all who are implicated. It may sound weird, but I hope you, too, (continue to) manage to find ways to feel small, and to integrate such practices of earthfulness into your own life. I hope you structurally gift yourself the time to let go, which is essential if you're to support others in doing the same.

So, the final questions I would like to close this chapter with are the following: How can I develop a practice that allows me to recharge and let go so that I can show up in service of the potential of the education system? And what must I (still) let go off in service of this potential?

With love,
Bas

"Love is the Bridge between you and everything"

Rumi

Notes

1. Van den Berg, B. (2023). *Design principles for regenerative higher education*. PhD dissertation, Wageningen School of Social Sciences, Wageningen University & Research. https://edepot.wur.nl/589879.
2. Bas is happy to share that a new master's programme set to launch in September of 2025 has gotten rid of a thesis entirely and can be successfully completed with a group-based project instead. Several undergraduate programmes are also experimenting with individual alternatives to graduation theses.
3. The ministry republished the materials two days later in slightly abbreviated form. While the content remained the same, they had added clearer disclaimers that these were not the official position of the government but the personal perspective of an academic.
4. Bas van den Berg published a book called *Onderwijzen tijdens transities*, in October 2023. The book launch was at a theatre called Pakhuis de Zwijger, in the centre of Amsterdam, which has a capacity of 330 guests. Van den Berg, B. (2023). *Onderwijzen tijdens transities*. Brave New Books.
5. The term acupuncture as a perspective in the transition literature emerged from the scholar Jessica Marie Hemingway. See, for example, Hemingway, J. M. (2024). Urban environmental acupuncture as a tool to support nature-based solution implementation: Does it deliver what it promises? *Urban Transformations, 6*(10).
6. Bas: I'd like to acknowledge the wonderful indirect contributions of two friends and experts in this matter. Dr. Kristina Bogner, who serves as an assistant professor at the University of Utrecht, and Femke Coops, who is an entrepreneur and PhD student at Eindhoven University of Technology. Their work and perspectives in emotions in transitional processes have had a profound impact on my thinking.
7. Bas: Although I believe we see similar dynamics in other transition arenas, which are fundamentally understudied.
8. See footnote above referring to the work of J. M. Hemingway
9. See, for example, the pivotal work of Capra, F., & Luisi, P. L. (2016). *The systems view of life – A unifying vision*. Cambridge University Press.
10. See Trungpa, C. (1984). *Shambhala: The sacred path of the warrior*. Shambhala Publications.
11. Bas: I've asked senior leaders to mentor me in this tension, and I engage with professional mental healthcare for my previously discussed depression.
12. Earthfulness is a term coined by Arjan Berkhuysen and Annemoon Elzinga, a couple who started engaging with the concept after the untimely passing of their son. They are currently developing Walks of Grief on the Dutch island of Terschelling. Earthfulness relates to daily practices of (re)connecting to the Earth.

13 See, for example, Notermans, I., von Wirth, T., & Loorbach, D. (2022). *An experiential guide for Transition Arenas*. DRIFT, Erasmus University Rotterdam.
14 Brown, B. (2021). *Atlas of the Heart: Mapping Meaningful Connection and the Language of Human Experience*. Vermillion Press.
15 Bas is happy to share that through intense therapy, lifestyle changes, and pharmacological interventions, the shadows are no longer dominant.
16 See, for example, May, K. (2020). *Wintering: The power of rest and retreat in difficult times*. Riverhead Books.

Section 2

Regenerative Educatorship

In this second half of this book, we turn our conversation more directly to the question of regenerative educatorship. What are we learning about what it means to regenerate ourselves and our education communities in pursuit of more life-affirming education potentialities? What key processes are involved? What capacities do we need to nurture? We wonder: Can we come up with some helpful premises, or perhaps even some frameworks, that can inspire and guide us?

To be honest, this feels like quite a challenge, and we're reminded, at this point, that we're not alone in this exploration. In many ways, we stand on the shoulders of giants, of all of those regenerative scholars and practitioners who paved the way. And just as important, as we are writing this book, we find ourselves part of a very engaged and inspiring community of like-minded educators, of peers. So, we've decided to design our harvesting process in strong engagement with both! In the next chapter – chapter 5 – we engage in a deep conversation with our peers from the Dutch Community of Practice Regenerative Education that we introduced in the beginning of the book, and that we've been part of since its start in 2021. Then, in chapter 6, we engage with regenerative framework thinking in the tradition of the Regenesis Institute for Regenerative Practice, to which we're deeply indebted in the development of this work. In doing so we are blessed with the resourcing of one of the Regenesis Institute's core faculty, Nicholas Mang, who has tremendously helped and encouraged us to present the premises that emerge from our work in dynamic and creative relationality to each other, in a way that invites, opens up, and is unfinished. After all this, we've got one last chapter in store for you, as we feel an urge to start as we began: with personal commitments and our collective invitation to you, dear reader. This time, rather than writing about why we embarked on this work, we write about how we've co-evolved with this book, and we express our hopes and intentions moving forward. Part of this, in fact, is an emerging School of Regenerative Educators, and we may just end up writing an epilogue after this third section of the book to say a bit more about this.

5 Stepping into Regenerative Educatorship

We are delighted to welcome some of our peers – Ingeborg, Daan, Michaela, Marlies, and Alette – into this chapter[1]. In a way, they've been there all along, for it's from our shared community of practice that this book project emerged in the first place, and they've been reading and thinking along from the start. In this chapter, we crank this co-creation up a notch, and to do so we invited them to a weekend retreat, in March 2024, in the wee village of Gouderak, near the famous place of origin of Gouda cheese and *stroopwafels*. At this point in time, we had a draft version of the first part of the book ready. We spent the first 1.5 days re-engaging with these chapters in close relation to participants' own experiences and practice. Our programme was infused by delicious vegan food, hikes, and yoga and mindfulness practices. All this paved the way for the 4-hour developmental fireplace conversation that forms the basis for this chapter, which we recorded in the afternoon of the second day. In this conversation, we zoomed in on our shared effort to 'step into regenerative educatorship'. What kind of process is this? What does it ask of us?

To support this conversation, we hung a framework on the wall (figure 3) that we refer to as the Regenerative Paths, or the three-fold path of regenerative educatorship. We developed this framework throughout the retreat as an attempt to gently remind all of us of a common thread that runs (at times quite explicitly) through all the chapters of this book, namely, that the process of regeneration is rather layered. In many ways, regenerating the education systems we are part of involves regenerating ourselves and how we work together as education actors. At times, this feels as if we're journeying along multiple paths at once – each with obstacles and beauties of their own – represented in the framework as the inner path, the communal path, and the whole-system path. It's tempting – perhaps especially so in modern western culture – to see these paths as separate or to prioritise one over the other. We propose, drawing on inspiration from ancient Celtic, Germanic, and Nordic representations of the geometric *triquetra* shape, that these paths are not separate at all, that they flow into, and pave the way for, each other. This was something we wanted to collectively hold in mind as we entered into the developmental conversation we are about to share.

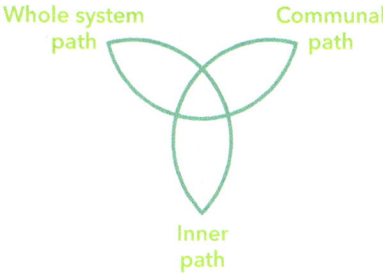

Figure 3: The Regenerative Paths.

Holding a Fireplace Conversation

In the middle of the room stands a small table. On it sit a burning candle, a singing bowl, and a small speaker radiating the crackling sound of a cosy fire. Around the table are three chairs positioned in a circle. One of these chairs is a bit more luxurious than the others, a bit more like a lazy armchair in which you think your best thoughts at the precipice of a deep sleep. This chair is called 'the hot seat', the seat for developing a new contribution to the conversation, a new perspective or emerging insight. The other two chairs are called 'resource seats'. Their *raison d'être* is to invite and help illuminate the full richness of the perspectives being developed in the hot seat. Behind these three chairs stand two couches and a couple of other chairs, together creating a second circle surrounding the first. This circle provides space to witness and collectively hold the energy field for the conversation that takes place in the inner circle.

Now, the way the fireplace conversation worked is as follows. First, we created some time and silence for imaging – an exercise you've seen us engage with several times throughout this book. This time, we gently invited each other to be with the first 1.5 days of the retreat through a guided meditation and to subsequently observe what images emerge around that core theme of 'stepping into regenerative educatorship', in silence. After 10 minutes or so, we struck the singing bowl standing on the table in the middle of the room and waited for its beautiful sound to fade. The conversation started when one of us – feeling ready to develop a first perspective – sat down in the hot seat and started speaking. From this moment onwards, the others – supporting the 'developer' in the hot seat with attention and compassion – were invited to take a seat in one of the resource chairs whenever they felt called to. Once the developer was done talking, the resourcers started actively helping the developer to explore further. Throughout the conversation of that afternoon, this kind of resourcing took various forms, like asking open questions, giving an encouraging nod, or sharing a short story or anecdote which could function to juxtapose or reinforce that which was coming forth in the conversation; in short, they acted in ways they felt were needed to support the process. Throughout the process, the witnesses, sitting in other chairs, were at all times free to move to and from the resource chairs, including by gently tapping someone occupying a resource seat on their shoulder to replace them. As this process went on for a while with the first developer, the conversation naturally reached a point of 'saturation'. At this point, the developer stood up, went back to the witness bench, and opened up space for a next person to move to the hot seat and bring something new into the conversation. Following this procedure, a rather intense, focused energy started forming, and it kept us going for four uninterrupted hours. Everyone took a turn occupying the hot seat. It felt quite magical to create such a focused and developmental energy together, and beyond the content of this chapter, we can really recommend this conversational and resourced method!

On the pages that follow, we present a condensed version of our fireplace conversation[2]. We purposely do not highlight who occupies what chair at what point in time. We do, however, highlight when a new person takes the hot seat to start developing a new perspective with a conversation header. We would now like to invite you to take a moment for some imaging before you read on, just as we ourselves did before we started the fireplace conversation.

Suggested Imaging
(see the "Textbox: A Practice of Imaging" in chapter 2 for a short elaboration on Imaging)

Gently hold on to the inner, communal, and whole-system paths of regeneration and your experience of working through the first section of the book. Now, what comes up if you image yourself taking a step forward within your education context to create space for regeneration?

Our Fireplace Conversation

The garden and the city

Hot Seat: I would like to kick off this conversation by sharing an image that I've been carrying with me for quite a while. A part of this image popped up recently during a training session for teachers within my university. In this session, we did a meditation exercise in which we were asked to look at Earth from a distance, imagine we were going to land on Earth for the first time, and then visualize what forms of education 'want to be birthed' on this precious planet. We were invited, in other words, to quite radically re-imagine the potential of education. The images that emerged for me were very playful and outdoors. I did not image school buildings but, rather, a more free, playful, immersed form of learning in and with nature. Now, as soon as we started imaging again just before this conversation, similar images started emerging again, and this time they reminded me of the garden of Eden, and the biblical story of how humanity left the garden of Eden and ended up living in a very special city. I mean, whether you're religious and of Christian faith or not, I think there is something very relatable in this story. It's about free, flourishing life (the garden) and organised, structured humanity (the city), and about the question of their relationship. You see, I think the crux of our work – and that is what my imaging was about – is to see the potential of both garden and city, of both human-made systems and freely flowing natural life. More specifically, I think regenerative education work is in many ways about how we can create 'garden-like qualities' from within the city. I see this as a lemniscate[3] (figure 4), where the potential of garden and city are interconnected, together resembling the ongoing challenge of living together, becoming more fully alive in relationship to each other, human and more-than-human.

Figure 4: A lemniscate.

Resource: The image that you are conjuring, for me, brings forth the perspective that we need to create that lemniscate ourselves, as an active process of self-and-world-making. We may have the tendency to move from one to the other, from city to garden, but you are arguing it is our role to bring the two worlds of garden and city together.

Hot Seat: Yes, exactly. This reminds me of work that I did long ago, in Lima, Peru. Lima, as perhaps you know, is located in the desert, and it is quite amazing to see how a big city and civilization developed in that context. My work there was to explore how forests could be nurtured into this desert city. During that process, at some point, one of the community elders became quite upset as they shared: 'Don't you know that all the green around here is our doing in the first place? We already birthed that, so what are you talking about? We are already bringing the forest in!' You see, I see quite clearly now that it is not about choosing one over the other, it's about their co-evolution, a point that's easy to miss when you enter, or look at, a space as an outsider. Yes, for me our contemporary education system resonates too strongly with the image of the high rises and concrete of the city. The call to purpose that I experience is to revitalise our relationship with the flow qualities of water, plants, and forests, and to bring these into the education system, to revitalise the city and, in doing so, revitalise ourselves.

Resource: Thank you for sketching this call to purpose so elegantly. I can imagine you are already trying to nurture this revitalization. How is it for you to engage with this work?

Hot Seat: My systemic role, especially now that I am in the later stages of my career, is mostly to create space for others to do this, creating space for young educators and students to create and nurture education informed by nature's wisdom. Doing so truly fulfils me; it's what keeps me going. Although, in all honesty, it is quite rare that the potential I see is truly fulfilled. I trust that the occasions in which it is are truly transformative for those involved. I trust that the encounter with a more 'enlivened' education space changes people. Recently, for instance, we organised a session with a local theatre group where our students were guided through creative forms of expression ending with a spoken word atelier. The spoken word performances had a magical and alchemical quality to them that made me go 'Wow'. It was awe inspiring, and the evening felt full of meaning and connection – an experience that truly felt to me like an entire summer youth camp was condensed into a single afternoon. It's perhaps just once in an entire academic year that I experience something like this, maybe twice if I'm lucky. But I have a deep sense of trust that these experiences awaken the life-giving force that is present in all of us and are deeply transformative for students and teachers alike. It's key that we create education conditions in which people can experience that they have life-giving force, that they can birth beauty, connection, regenerative change.

Steadfastly coming from love

Hot Seat: I decided to take the hot seat next, as I sense that what I want to bring in builds strongly on what we just called 'the life-giving force inside us all'. When I was imaging prior to this conversation, two words intuitively popped up. The words *strong love*. Now, I know that *love* is a loaded word, with myriad interpretations and associations, but I sense that there is something powerful in using this word, that love lies at the heart of regenerative practices, of regenerative educatorship.

For I think it's quite accurate to say that 'to love' another human being, nature, community, or even 'the world' means to be devoted to the life-giving force that resides in each of us, and that is all around. It means that you believe in, and are mesmerised by, the potential of unique beings and communities to flourish, to reveal themselves, as themselves. It means deeply believing in the intrinsic value of all life, and a desire for all of us to experience the fullness of our being as we are immersed in the world together. And, therefore, a disposition towards care and compassion, a dedication to the wellbeing and thriving of those we find ourselves entangled with[4]. I think, as educators aspiring to walk a regenerative path, we are driven by this love. We are driven by love for our students, our colleagues, the Earth, and we want to allow it to guide our actions. This is where the second word comes in: *strong*. You see, I think the biggest challenge we face might not be to experience this love – I think many people already strongly do so – but to develop the strength, the steadfastness, to truly let it guide our actions. To be, in a way, uncompromising, not accepting it if others' life-giving forces are denied existence. Daring to make choices, to say no, to no longer do something when our love demands so, even, or perhaps especially, when this means challenging the status quo, standing out.

Developing that capacity for 'strong love' is a challenging developmental process. Especially because it is very tempting to lose sight of a nested, integral perspective, a perspective of simultaneous love for oneself, the human and more-than-human other, and the bigger wholes we are part of. I think this resonates quite strongly with the stories developed in section 1 of the book. Perhaps particularly chapter 4, in which Bas's story made me aware that it is quite possible to 'break through doors' out of love for one's students and for the Earth, but that if you're not careful about your own and your colleagues' needs in the process – if you're not strong enough in practicing loving yourself and your peers – this is a dangerous business. I mean, there are so many examples of idealistic people having burnouts, to give just one example. So, yes, I think regenerative educatorship entails practising strong love in an integral way. It includes accepting that you cannot do everything, remaining humble and kind at heart, and yet being purposeful and determined in doing what you can do in the name of love.

Resource: I decided to sit here because you're talking about love. Just yesterday, in conversation with some of you, I found myself talking about the relationship between love and pain. The moment we start to love, and through that to become alive, is also the moment we start to experience pain. The moment we start to look at something or someone with love is the moment we start to see their pain. And the moment we see pain, we tend to step back. How does that resonate with you?

Hot Seat: I think you're saying something very important. And perhaps my first response is that it is not just pain that we start seeing and feeling. It's also potential, and joy. This goes hand in hand, right? Once we start seeing another being with love, we see the pain and we see the joy, we see the danger and we see the potential. And we feel this deep inclination to serve the unfolding of potential rather than to be complicit to the infliction of pain. But, yes, we need to learn to be with the pain as well. In a certain way, if we want to work regeneratively in education, we need to hold space for experiencing the pain that comes with seeing that things we love are suffering or are at risk. And we need to find ways to not be stifled by this experience, to use it constructively. I mean, it's certainly not a good excuse to not love, right?

Resource: Yes, I recognize that I sometimes perhaps focus too much on pain, because it is my perspective that we tend to neglect pain, suffering, decay, and death within our society, causing even more pain. It is just part of life, like everything else. Perhaps the question I'm also trying to raise is how much love a space or a person can handle. For instance, I was recently teaching a class where I knew someone was going through grief over a lost relative, and out of care, I asked how they were coping. They started to cry. But they hadn't shared what they were going through yet with the rest of the class, who witnessed this moment, and afterwards I wasn't sure if I had done the right thing. Sometimes, we may need to restrain ourselves as the other may not, at that moment, be ready to receive the love and care we want to express.

Hot Seat: Hmm, yes, I reckon you are right. But, were you to have restrained yourself in this particular example out of a concern for the 'readiness' of this student, would that in itself not have been an act of love as well? Is consciously practising restraint not one of the prominent ways in which we express love? I'm reminded of how Koen described his interaction with one of the students he supervised in chapter 3, in terms of offering resistance. He sensed that, presented with an opportunistic and relatively easy opportunity to shape her thesis project around installing solar energy panels, the student in question was tempted to leave her initial passion for care work behind. Koen could have been very direct in this particular moment, saying 'No, I don't approve of this direction; stick to your initial motivation', and it is quite possible that this would have inflicted harm on his relationship with the student. But he also didn't just move along. He resisted her in a more subtle way, sharing his observation calmly, inviting her to take some time to reflect, and keeping her in the lead of the decision process. So, I guess what I'm saying is that part of acting out of love is to approach the other as being in charge of their own process, in terms of both its speed and its direction, and that often entails restraining oneself.

Resource: I want to invite you to develop the perspective of 'steadfastness' a bit further. What does it mean, what does it look like? And also, I'm curious if you can say something about the potential of 'strong love' to be a reconciling force.

Hot Seat: Thanks for these questions. This really helps! I'm becoming aware now that this notion of being steadfast or strong in our love conjures different images for me. One of them, which may be counterintuitive, is not doing, letting go. We normally associate being strong with doing something, like lifting weights or making a grand gesture. But I think often not doing is key as well. Being part of the contemporary education system, it is often much harder for me to stop doing things that – seen through the lens of love – make no sense, than it is to shape new initiatives I feel enthusiastic about. So, I'm talking about those moments when you intuitively feel that 'This doesn't really make sense' or 'This doesn't really work'. Being steadfast in your love might mean to simply permit yourself to say 'Fine, then I won't do it'. However, and perhaps this is where the question about reconciliation comes in, there is of course the risk that when we're continuously and radically steadfast like this, we end up being spit out by the system, we end up alienated. So, I reckon using 'strong love' as a compass doesn't just imply being uncompromising. The compass is that we want to serve the unfolding of the potential of those we love, to do what needs to be done to nurture the life-giving forces of those in the education contexts we work in. In other words, we need to 'stay there', we need to stay in the relationship and avoid alienating ourselves through radical stubbornness. Perhaps this is part of the artistry of regenerative educatorship, sensing just how radical or disruptive to be when and where. And I think one of our first responsibilities as regenerative educators is to find places where we actually feel like we can do this, where we can 'stay in the relationship' or as Donna Haraway would say 'stay with the trouble'[5].

Resource: I have been sitting with a question, a care, a challenge for a while now that relates strongly to this unfolding conversation. What if strong love is not enough? What if strong love goes so far beyond what the system is able to accept that it cannot allow the system to exist within itself?

Hot Seat: The very honest, and perhaps also a bit harsh, answer that I feel emerging as you ask this is: 'Then so be it'. I mean, 'loving relationships' are not a means to an end to me but an end themselves. I'm not willing to say, 'Ooh, acting out of love is not possible, so let's just forget about it'. I mean, if it were true that there is no place for love in education systems, I'd probably choose not to work in them and would look for other, more welcoming places. But I am far from believing that, and if you walk around in schools and universities, the evidence that this is indeed not true is everywhere. But perhaps your question also relates to something else, which I hear a lot. Namely: Is love enough to save the world? Is love a good enough answer to all the atrocities in the world? Is it enough to save the Earth? Intuitively I want to counter those questions by saying, 'What if it is the only viable answer?...' But in all honesty, I don't know. What I can say is that I struggle with the idea of saving the world to begin with, and that I've seen too many examples of people neglecting their own boundaries while attempting to do so. And who knows what kind of unintended side-effects that has? For me, being an expression of love, and fostering relationships driven by love, is enough of a 'victory' in and of itself, and I trust that using this as my compass will enable me to offer a meaningful contribution to the world-in-becoming.

To be an enlightening resource

Hot Seat: Building on the previous two contributions, I want to develop some thoughts about educating as 'shining a light on potential'[6], and about what this entails in terms of our own 'visibility' and role as educators. I was quite touched when we spoke earlier about the exemplary experience of the spoken word atelier, where students became visible with their life-giving force. This is not the type of visibility that we usually see on social media. It's not complying with what society expects us to be; it's more authentic self-expression in relation to the world. And as we were talking, I was reminded of an invitation Kurt Vonnegut wrote to his students at 84 years of age[7]. In this invitation, he requests from his students that throughout their lives, they continue to engage in a search for themselves. As part of this letter, he invited them to create a poem that included a piece of themselves, and to then tear it up in a thousand pieces and gift it back to the world. The reward for the poem is not in being seen, it is in that you 'have experienced becoming, learning a lot more about what's inside you, and you made your own soul grow'. I found this gesture utterly beautiful. It made me increasingly aware that there is such a core discrepancy for me between how we, as regenerative educators, aspire to enlighten the life-giving potential of our students and the kind of societal performing that we mostly request of them instead.

Resource: I really get what you are saying. The reason I took a seat on this chair is that I wanted to truly see you. I think the strong love that we just discussed also implies the ability to truly see, to enlighten the potential that is there but may not yet be manifest. When the education programme I work for grew in size, I shared with my colleagues that I found it essential that each of our students is truly seen by at least one teacher. Also, in our programme we try to depart from the question 'What is the unique potential of each student?' – to shine a light on their core being. Looking at someone's potential, seeing what may manifest. How does that resonate with the perspective of enlightening that you so beautifully put forward, and what does it mean for you to bring this enlightening act into practice?

Hot Seat: Interestingly, as an educator, I experience that to truly see the other I often have to stop conforming to the societal pressure of being seen myself. I mean, as educators we like to be visible, don't we? We like to take the stage and be in charge. But by stepping back, by no longer worrying about my own visibility, I can create the space for others to show themselves, to be seen. Because I spend less energy on being visible, there is more space to let others' unique potential be truly seen. My ability to let go of my desire to be seen, to fill the space, is a life-giving force that enables me to truly see others. In a sense, this is what it means to step into an education space as a resource, as someone standing in service of the potential of others.

Resource: I feel a need to highlight something I find profoundly beautiful in the perspective on being a resource that you're developing here: creating space for the other to emerge by removing elements of your own presence that do not need to be there. Yet you're not talking about fully removing yourself. Within that space you create, you are speaking of your own role as one of enlightening and resourcing. An inviting force. A loving presence. It's like by becoming less visible in ways you actually don't find super helpful, you also create space for yourself to become visible in a different, perhaps more regenerative way!

Hot Seat: Interesting, perhaps an example would be good after all. A while ago, I was asked to step into the role of process guide for the development of a new curriculum for one of our education programs. At some point in the process that followed, part of the development team went to the director behind my back to say they had lost confidence in my ability to guide this collective process. This led to the director calling me and telling me that I would be removed from this role. However, at the same time, the development team and my director valued my expertise, and they asked me to remain part of the developmental team. Initially, I felt like I had been stabbed in the back, by a team that I thought I had built a relationship of trust with yet that chose to go to our director behind my back. The day after this happened, I sat down with the entire team and I shared my sadness about how things had unfolded. In that moment, a space opened up, a space for emotions that had been held back in the shadows up to that moment in time. Not just my own, but of the whole team. This simultaneously helped me to step out of the spotlight of process guide and stay connected to the ongoing developmental project, to step into the process again as a team member. Stepping back from my role as process guide enabled me to show up in a different way and allowed the enlightening of emotions that needed to become visible for the sake of the greater whole, and after this we felt ready to move on as a team.

Resource: I sense a connection between this unfolding conversation and the previous one, about lovingly stepping into education spaces. As you mention, even despite initially experiencing 'being stabbed in the back', you chose a reconciling pathway to move forward. I want to invite you to look at this experience as a loving act of relating to the potential of place.

Hot Seat: Thank you. I looked with love at my colleagues because I could sense how much they cared about the potential of what we were working on. They shared a strong sense of purpose about what we were working on. Sensing that potential and purpose helped me to find that reconciling path. And also, I sensed that I still had a contribution to give – and therefore it felt like an act of love both towards myself and towards the project to renew my role in the team, rather than to step away out of frustration or anger or whatnot.

The mighty swan and the ugly duckling

Hot Seat: I'm bursting to talk about something that's been building up throughout this conversation. I mean, to be steadfast in your love, to show up as a resource, to shape your actions in relation to the potential of place ... that requires so much courage[8]! The courage of letting your unique qualities shine for a more regenerative pathway for the whole you are part of. I mean, that's hard! For me, it's quite relatable to let my own qualities shine in front of direct colleagues or my students, but I observe that I find this a lot harder in relationship to the larger whole, to 'step up' in relationship to institutional dynamics and processes, to speak my voice in the larger system. I feel like I sometimes lack that courage. It's not easy to acknowledge or share that.

Resource: First of all, I think it's very courageous that you just sit down and share this challenge with us. You mention that you find it harder to be courageous in relationship with the larger education system than with your colleagues or students. Do you know where that difficulty comes from?

Hot Seat: That's an interesting question. During the imaging exercise we did prior to this conversation, what came up was something that I have felt more often. I was imaging myself as a mighty swan, but simultaneously I caught myself not truly believing that image, feeling more like the metaphorical ugly duckling. There is an insecurity that I feel when I engage with larger systemic change which I don't experience when I'm working to change something in the program I'm part of. But when I look deep inside myself, what I want to bring into the world of education requires a profound courage. Of course, it's beautiful and important to focus on my own programme, but when I consider the potential of education systems, I do sense a will to think bigger. My own projection of the ugly duckling, which is strong, holds me back from stepping into a more systemic role.

Resource: Well, I think I speak for many when I say you aren't the only one who is held back by some of our internal images of our own potential. What would the potential of stepping beyond the image of the ugly duckling be? And what would it mean to step beyond this image in a loving and life-giving way?

Hot Seat: I know, I can't transform the education system by myself, yet I do see an empowering role for myself if I do step into it with courage. The image that comes up for me is one of a bright diamond that reflects light on others, inviting them to fulfil their own potential in service of the regeneration of the education system they are part of.

Resource: Were there moments where you thought 'If only I had been more courageous'?

Hot Seat: Well, we are currently working on curriculum redevelopment in my institute. I shared Bas's recently published book[9] with our education manager, but what I actually wanted to do was say 'Hey, let's invite Bas to help us to look at the regenerative potential of our curriculum'. But I didn't do that. I only shared the book. I felt like the ugly duckling trying to speak up rather than the mighty swan saying what she has to say. I can feel the power of the swan, its steadfastness and determination, as we discussed. I feel it's there, but I also feel like I don't always live up to its potential, and that saddens me. There is this speech by Nelson Mandela where he talks about how our biggest fear is ourselves. 'Our deepest fear is not that we are inadequate. Our deepest fear is that we are powerful beyond measure'[10]. How we make ourselves too small while we are actually large and mighty and powerful.

Resource: If I make it really small and I see that mighty swan standing in front of a programme director, what is it that holds you back, that scares you? What could happen if you suggest, 'Let's invite an outside expert'?

Hot Seat: I mean, nothing concrete, like 'Oh, she'll think I'm stupid', or anything like that. I tend to see a lot of obstacles in situations like this. Like 'It's too short notice; we already have strict deadlines'. Yet the swan in me doesn't let this stop her; she accepts that not everything I bring forth will be actualised but doesn't let this hold her back.

Resource: It's a privilege to be a witness to this showcase of what courage is, or what it looks like. Of how you're already courageous enough to live a large part of your potential yet simultaneously feel the pain of sensing that you could live it more fully. This conjures the image for me of courage as a journey, and of potential as a journey. As a lifelong process.

Hot Seat: A lifelong process it is for sure, in the sense that I feel like 'swan-ness' is something that needs to be remembered, accomplished, time and again. But at the same time, I feel like for the mighty swan courage is not gradually at all, not something that needs to be collected, more like an absolute state of being. The mighty swan is courageous, fearless, steadfast. That is her essence. So, if I speak from the perspective of the ugly duckling, I have to continuously climb giant mountains to muster up the courage to offer my contribution. But when I manage to remember the mighty swan in myself, when I connect to my inner swan-ness, it's just a matter of being who I am. For me, this feels like a type of inner sensitisation with the world around me. And it is something that I can practice by being present and compassionate. By loving the ugly duckling in myself, who is also part of me, and in fact maybe not so ugly after all, and carries the swan within her at all times.

Collectively holding space

Hot Seat: I love how this conversation is exploring the depths of the inner work involved in stepping into regenerative educatorship. In a way, I feel like in our shared space here, in this two-day retreat, we support and resource each other, we are able to articulate what this work entails for us. I'd like to develop the importance and value of that communal dimension a bit further, which is exactly what I saw in my own imaging at the start of this conversation. I saw a community gently and tenderly working on a collective bit of art – everyone working together as one to give life to beauty. That image warms my soul. And it's how this very conversation, and being part of regenerative education communities more generally, feels to me: a loving connecting around a collective developmental question, around a shared potential.

Resource: I'm happy that you're inviting us to turn our gaze towards how nurturing regenerative educatorship really is a communal effort. To invite you to develop this perspective further, perhaps I can share something I've been thinking about throughout this conversation. I've been thinking, namely, that implicitly 'judging' has been a central theme in our conversation. In how we talk about love, visibility and courage, I feel like we're moving towards a more compassionate, open stance towards ourselves and towards each other. A resourcing stance. Which feels so much in contrast to how, in the education system, we are constantly expected to judge students, ourselves, each other. I am very curious how you see this, and how it relates to the kind of regenerative community you speak of.

Hot Seat: Yeah, this resonates strongly with me, and it relates to something that, inspired by the work of Carol Sanford[11], has become somewhat of a mission to me: to speak up whenever I hear the word 'feedback'. I'm also reminded of a recent book launch where one of the speakers mentioned how siloed and compartmentalised education has become. And how assessment plays a dominant role. I mean, it's not just that we assess our students all the time, often in rather impersonal ways. It's also that we continuously ask our students to assess us and that we're regularly assessing each other as colleagues. I sense so much toxicity in all of that. I mean, there is so much judgement but often much less resourcing, much less truly seeing each other and standing side by side. To me, this truly feels like a nodal point of pain in the education system, and I think it requires collective action. We need to come together differently as an education community to create space for the love, connection, and courage we've been speaking of.

Resource: Where do you see the potential for reconciliation from this perspective?

Hot Seat: So, I think that potential lies in finding liminality, like the guerrilla gardening we discussed earlier in the book. If we look at education as the high rises of the concrete city, it's not that easy to just whip out a tile and start a garden. You need a collective to work together on nourishing the capacity to reconnect with living systems. I think the reconciling force is trying not to stand against the education system but wondering, from a steadfast love, 'Okay, but what can we do together?' That feels a bit naughty, in a way. Through collective naughtiness we may be able to co-create and nourish emergent guerrilla gardens. That's also the power I see in the work of Carol Sanford. She embodies that type of naughty wisdom to invite the potential of systems quite strongly for me.

Resource: Can you explore how to engage with this potential with others a bit further?

Hot Seat: I think this relates to collectively carrying the responsibility of holding and creating spaces where potential for the greater whole can flourish. It starts by acknowledging that a shared pole star exists. If I may, I would like to connect this to the magic that I have seen emerge in co-creative spaces with students.

It is the active choice of stepping back as an educator so that students can step forward and co-create an education space with me that makes a profound difference. This fundamentally and intentionally breaks through the hierarchy we generally experience in education spaces. With that we can create brave spaces for experimentation, spaces where we may find paths to reconcile with some of the expectations of the system. Of course this kind of experimentation is always risky, but taking those risks as a collective, and carefully holding space for experimentation and connection for all involved, can create so much aliveness. For a number of years now, I have been surprised by what students are able to bring into such spaces. And I'm aware that this surprise on my behalf still reveals a hierarchical lens, an a priori judgement or expectation of what students are supposed or able to do. I'm also becoming increasingly aware that this collective holding of space opens up potential for a more critical edge, for asking each other more difficult or painful questions, and for welcoming a wider range of emotions – that it invites and enables us to not walk away when things get harder. A collective or community that is truly engaged with regenerative education embodies this willingness to stay with the trouble.

Resource: Hmm, this deeply interests me. I mean, perhaps sometimes we might create the impression, or hold the desire, of regenerative education as something rosy and smooth. But as you frame it now, if we come from a place of love and connection, we in fact open up space for the hard stuff. Quite like how we earlier spoke of pain as being closely linked to love. What comes up for me now is that this collectively held space you speak of invites us to be more honest, more open towards what is. Even if this means asking difficult or critical questions of each other or facing difficult emotions. I'm wondering, what does it mean to co-create communities in which this kind of openness is a core value?

Hot Seat: I reckon this radical openness often starts with yourself. I mean, you cannot really expect others to be open towards you if you're not willing to move towards openness yourself. This certainly requires a lot of inner development, as well embodiment in, for example, what stories we choose to tell. I think that quality is also present in this book. Take, for example, the opening letters. In a way, this book starts with radical openness, and I think that this is far from a coincidence. But 'me being radically open' is, simultaneously, not enough. I mean, just as when we spoke about love, sometimes restraint is also needed. I can also be too open or too personal. I feel like the art is to collectively 'spiral' into increasing openness. With each community, it's contextual, and it needs time. I think there is something like the art of gently leaning into openness while building a community's capacity to engage with radical openness. I mean, I think the regenerative path is more of a soft evolution than a hard revolution. Its intention is not to violently break down 'what is' but to approach it from a position of love and act towards its potential to evolve.

Being in between

Hot Seat: I'm very inspired by the direction this conversation is taking now, the direction of 'the soft evolution'. And although the intention here is explicitly different from 'the hard revolution', I want to explore how the soft evolution, too, comes with the natural death of things. How dying is part of evolution. And how it's very hard to be with this reality and to approach it with care. This relates, also, to my own imaging prior to this conversation. In it, I felt like being trapped in a tall, dark building that was collapsing on top of me. This is quite a dark image, which links to my own developmental journey in life. I mean, I've felt like that for a long time, and I think many people feel like this in processes of education system change. It took me a long time – in life, and in my imaging – to find my footing, to let go of the crumbling support walls around me, the walls from which I used to draw strength. So, as we engage in this soft evolution, we need to acknowledge that we are attached to the structures that are evolving, and just like in chapter 4 of the book, I have been thinking about this in the context of hospicing – the caring act of facilitating the dying of some of the elements of how education systems work right now, and the profound fear that this often releases.

Resource: The building that, in your imaging, is collapsing on top of you raises the regenerative question 'How can we take many of the elements discussed here today to help people move through that experience of collapse?' How can we help each other to see the potential? How can we actually achieve that shared experience of a soft evolution, rather than a life-threatening collapse? Does that resonate with you?

Hot Seat: It does, but I think it's important to be aware that this kind of evolution is not a straightforward process. Often, I need 'times of in betweenness', times in which I already let go of the old, accept that certain things don't work for me anymore, but cannot yet see the new. Between dying and new life there are times of open space, silence, of not knowing – the space which is required for something new to be birthed. This is a space I find difficult to be with. I see this, for instance, in the profound discomfort many of us feel with long silences in conversation, or in how we teach, for that matter. But it is in silence that space is created for new things to emerge. So, hospicing is not just about helping each other to see that the building collapsing is part of a necessary evolutionary process, but also about embracing the interbellum between death and new life, allowing ourselves to spend some time in between. About embracing the silence so that from it new potential can emerge.

Resource: This is so recognizable…. I mean, take how we tend to shape education in the face of ecological collapse in today's education systems. Educators tend to be mostly preoccupied with finding 'ways out', finding answers. It often requires a strong effort and resistance to give yourself – and your colleagues and students – permission to be with the grief, the silence, the in betweenness of hospicing, too. But doing so is actually so important, such an integral part of the regenerative process.

Hot Seat: Yeah, and again, this takes courage. Do you, when these moments of in betweenness present themselves, however short they are, have the courage to see them and to stay in them? Or do you resist and hang on? The poems 'Dear Darkening Ground' by Rilke[12] and 'How to Be Alone' by Pádraig Ó Tuama[13] capture these difficulties beautifully for me. And in a way, to me, this conversation embodies this quality. We created a space for a conversation where none of us knew where it would go, while knowing that this is key to allowing anything new to emerge. This requires a radical trust in silence, and in the process of emergence.

Playfully going forth as constructive disruptors

Hot Seat: As we're slowly coming to an end of this conversation, I feel like ending with some of the naughty and playful energy that popped up in this conversation when we spoke of guerrilla gardening. You know, navigating between the regenerative work I want to do, and do well, and what the system asks of me is not easy. It feels a bit like walking on a tightrope. And I often don't feel like I have enough time to do everything I want to do well. So, I am looking for a way to be a constructive disruptor without being spit out by the system. And I notice that this perspective of playfulness, or naughtiness, really helps me. It doesn't always have to be super serious and hard; it can also be enjoyable to play this game, to walk on the rope. For instance, I remember a particular innovator whose approach was to ask 'dumb' questions all the time to trigger people to reflect on why things are the way they are.

Resource: Yeah, indeed, developing our own and the system's capacity to engage with constructive disruption might be a core process in system regeneration.

Hot Seat: Yes, and I notice that throughout this conversation I'm becoming increasingly willing to take on the mantle of a constructive disruptor myself. Articulating this intention makes me feel quite happy and joyful. Like I'm ready to disrupt next week, and to enjoy it! You know, given that we tend to take the systems we're part of so seriously, I feel like it creates space if you have the ability to engage naughtily, from a position of strong love, and question what is going on. I mean, let's be real, if you don't put your grades in the system in the third week after a test but instead in the fourth week, is that really the end of the world? Of course not.

Resource: I heard you mention that you often experience you do not have the time to engage with the work you want to do.

Hot Seat: I mean, you choose what you invest time in. The last few weeks I have been taking more time for some of our master's students who were working on their graduation projects. I thought I noticed in one of our meetings that they felt abandoned and would appreciate it if we met more often, even though according to the system I didn't have the time to do so. We ended up working together every week for more than a month while none of us had dedicated time for it. Just being there, and holding a space, which they lovingly filled with apple pie, allowed them all to work more constructively on their graduation. It didn't even feel like I was overworking; in fact, it revitalised me. So, I just did it. I intend to say yes more often in these kind of moments. But in the highly structured and pre-planned environment I am part of this also means I have been unable to finish certain other tasks which were assigned to me. Tasks I didn't prioritize, and tasks that didn't feel meaningful to me. Instead of stressing over this 'failure' or feeling guilty, I now see this is an act of constructive disruption. I prioritised the need of my students over tasks I didn't see the meaning of. To be honest, I'm quite enjoying the way that makes me feel. Ha!

Notes

1. This chapter was co-created with Ingeborg Heezen, Daan Buijs, Michaela Hordijk, Marlies van der Wee-Bedeker, and Alette Los, members of the Dutch Community of Practice Regenerative Education.
2. The resulting text was reshared with those who participated in the fireplace conversation, and after some back-and-forth fine-tuning, everyone approved the final version shared here.
3. The lemniscate is one of the archetypical forms for endless renewal and regeneration, where the middle represents a crossing, or connection, between two parts of a whole – like inner and outer development, as we have been talking about throughout the book. Or, as framed here, as two parts of reality – garden and city, freedom and structure. The lemniscate invites us to not get stuck on one side (in this case 'the structured city' or 'the free garden') but, rather, to see the whole and seek ways for energy to flow from side to side, and for the potential this opens up.
4. We are aware that this is a particular way to speak about love. Although we do not follow a specific school or tradition here – and we encourage exploring the concept of love through your own lenses and experiences – we would like to share a few sources that continue to inspire us. In many ways, the philosophy of love has its roots in the four Ancient Greek concepts of love – *storge*, *philia*, *eros*, and *agape* (see, for instance, *The Four Loves* by C. S. Lewis). Perhaps an ecologically informed agape – an unconditional, deep reverence and love for all life – comes closest to the love we are talking about. Co-founder of Schumacher College Satish Kumar recently wrote a beautiful book that resonates strongly with this. This is a book we wholeheartedly recommend. We also find inspiration in Hannah Arendt's well-known work on 'amor mundi' (love for the world), as it embodies clearly the notion that to love an other – and the world at large – is to embrace difference and plurality, and to be devoted to each other's opportunity to live a full life in a shared world. And Arendt, too, reminds us that true love is unconditional; you don't stop loving your child when they misbehave, and neither should we stop loving the world because it is full of destruction and injustice. Quite the opposite: Our ability to love is the very source of our ability to take shared responsibility for a better world. And, to conclude this footnote, we also find ourselves moved by more spiritual musings of love, such as those widely available by mystic and poet Rumi. His work shares the same commitment to love integrally – to love all life – and a similar realism in that loving something means opening oneself to its true nature and unique potential and aliveness, and a deep inclination to serve it. In his musings, we also recognise the notion – which we experience to be very true ourselves – that loving ourselves and loving the world are non-separable, and that as we work through our own internal barriers or traumas, our capacity to love tends to grow in all directions. Lewis, C. S. (1960). *The Four Loves.* Geoffrey

	Bles; Kumar, S. (2023). *Radical love – From separation to connection with the Earth, each other, and ourselves.* Parallax Press. Arendt, H. (1961) (Ed.). *Between past and future: Six exercises in political thought.* Faber and Faber.
5	See Haraway, D. J. (2016). *Staying with the trouble: Making kin in the Chthulucene.* Duke University Press.
6	This links strongly to an ancient education debate about the etymological roots of the word education, and whether it derives from *educare* (to mold or to train) or from *educere* (to draw out).
7	While the original location the letter that was uploaded can no longer be found, the letter is widely available online and absolutely worth reading as an example of grace in eldership.
8	The 'Hot Seat' specified that their perspective was heavily informed by the School voor Zijnsoriëntatie, see www.zijnsorientatie.nl.
9	Bas's book on educating during transitions is referenced here. Van den Berg, B. (2023). *Onderwijzen tijdens transities.* Brave New Books.
10	Bas's book on educating during transitions is referenced here. Van den Berg, B. (2023). Onderwijzen tijdens transities. Brave New Books.
11	This refers to Sanford, C. (2019). *No more feedback: Cultivate consciousness at work.* Interoctave.
12	https://www.youtube.com/watch?v=GjGCm_0kVok
13	https://www.youtube.com/watch?v=HgZT6UJocRs

Intermezzo
Storying Your Own Regenerative Educatorship

In the first section of this book, we explored three of our own unfolding stories of trying to think and act regeneratively within education systems. In these chapters, each story focused on the relationships we as educators have with students (chapter 2), our colleagues (chapter 3), and the larger system(s) of which we are part (chapter 4). These stories contain various themes – such as belonging, loving resistance, co-creation, community building, purpose, steadfastness, constructive disruption, hospicing, care, systemic acupuncture, and several more. In chapter 5, we explored these themes in more depth through a fireplace conversation. In the chapter that follows, we'll integrate what we've been learning about what it means, and takes, to regenerate our education roles, practices, and systems in three regenerative frameworks. But before we go there, we would like to invite you to explore a story of your own. A story that may contain similar themes as the ones we have explored so far, but that may also weave yet other themes into your experience of working with this book.

Below, we present a set of questions that mirror the kinds of resourcing questions we asked each other throughout this book. These questions are designed to elicit and deepen your innate ability to reflect on the roles you currently play in relation to the regeneration of education practices and / or systems. These are questions you can engage with over and over, and your answers are likely to shift over time and between projects and contexts.

Think of a project or experience in which you play(ed) an active role that – for you – was at least somewhat part of 'the regenerative current'. If none come to mind, think of a project that you would like to have become regenerative. We purposefully restrain ourselves from offering a set of criteria in this intermezzo of what qualifies as such a project or experience, and we invite you to think/feel for yourself after having read the first part of this book. If you have a project or experience in mind, we invite you to engage with the following questions, either individually or with peers, in a way that you see fit. It may help you to transform your reflections into a letter similar to the one we opened the book with, while keeping a particular recipient or audience in mind (which could well be yourself).

- What are you trying to regenerate, and for whom (e.g. yourself, students, colleagues, a larger education or societal community, a place)? How would you formulate your more specific regenerative aims? What makes these aims regenerative? And why do you care so much about them?
- What does it ask from you to show up and act in congruence with these aims? How does/could this play out in terms of how you engage in relationships with your students, your colleagues, and/or the system(s) you are part of?
- How do/could you develop and nourish the capacity inside yourself to show up and act in these ways? What is resourcing you? And can you sense a developmental potential for yourself, your community, and the larger system you are part of?

6 Thinking Regeneratively About Educatorship

In the five chapters that preceded this one, we've engaged with the phenomenon of regenerative educatorship in depth. In this chapter, we want to introduce three systemic frameworks that dynamically bring together the main themes and insights that we've been exploring along the way. These frameworks do not offer step-by-step instructions as to what to do to develop your own regenerative educatorship. They're more like a thinking technology, a way to systematically challenge how we think about what we experience and do, and an invitation to explore (more) regenerative ways of being and acting. The names of the three frameworks (figure 5) are:

1. Regenerative Paths;
2. Regenerative Virtues; and
3. Regenerative Capabilities.

Indeed, the first one you've already come across, in chapter 5, but we will re-iterate it here because we find that these three frameworks best come to life in relation to each other. So, without further delay, let us show you all three together:

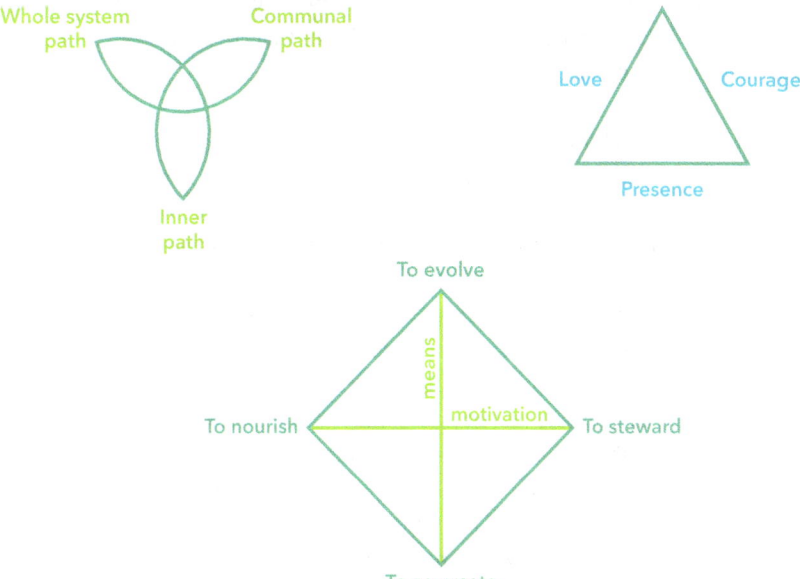

Figure 5: The three frameworks of regenerative educatorship; top left: Regenerative Paths; top right: Regenerative Virtues; bottom: Regenerative Capabilities.

Creating Systemic Frameworks

We are quite impatient to get into each framework in detail, but first it's important to share with you how we went about creating them. To start with, we drew heavily on a tradition of living systems frameworks, in close proximity to the work of the Regenesis Institute of Regenerative Development. In this tradition, the three geometrical shapes that we use – a triquetra (i.e. Regenerative Paths), a triad (i.e. Regenerative Virtues), and a tetrad (i.e. Regenerative Capabilities) – each have their own intrinsic quality. As we mentioned in chapter 5, a triquetra illustrates different dimensions or levels of reality which are deeply and dynamically interconnected as they flow into each other in a never-ending developmental process. As such, a triquetra serves to move beyond black or white discussions across competing theories of how things change (e.g. does change come from above or from below?) and to provide a more holistic way of thinking, being and doing. Building on this, we use the triquetra shape to offer our interpretation of how the journey of regenerative educatorship comprises multiple interrelated paths that each deserve our recognition and attention.

Our inspiration for using frameworks comes more directly from working with those developed by the Regenesis Institute. Following their work, which in turn is inspired by ancient wisdoms and perspectives, we understand the quality of a triad to be to set an energy field. Each 'leg' of a triad represents something crucial that's inherent to a certain activity or space – a certain quality to uphold, to live up to. We use a triad to offer our interpretation of the core virtues that regenerative education stories and experiences radiate. A tetrad is complementary to a triad. We understand the quality of a tetrad to be to structure a sustained activity or project. Each point of a tetrad portrays a certain dimension of an activity that's important for its fulfilment and remains dynamically related to the other dimensions. We therefore use a tetrad to offer our interpretation of the core capabilities that co-constitute the practice of regenerative educatorship.

Let us move on to how we crafted the frameworks more concretely. In chapter 5, we already described this for the Regenerative Paths, and we'd like to do the same for the Regenerative Virtues and the Regenerative Capabilities. To do so, we need to bring you along to the artist village of Bergen, in the north-west of the Netherlands. (Not to be confused with the artistic and much more famous city of Bergen in Norway, which was a mistake Bas made, and he almost went there instead.) Just before the 2024 summer break, we travelled to Sofia's temporary home in Bergen for two full days dedicated to working on this chapter. The three of us had been rereading earlier chapters and imaging what this chapter could look like. In our conversations with Nicholas Mang – our developmental editor from the Regenesis Institute – we'd started talking about developing a tetrad framework, but a triad was not yet clearly in our minds. On the afternoon of the first day in Bergen, after some preparatory work, we went on a long hike in the forest and dunes and started recording our conversation. At some point, we ended up in an open field, and there we started drawing a large tetrad in the sand. We decided to literally walk through it together and talk about what each part felt like, what it stood for, and how it related to the earlier chapters. We repeated this exercise the next day to create more depth and to fine-tune our choice of words. This is how the Regenerative Capabilities tetrad-shaped framework was developed, and the way we present it in what follows is based on our recorded conversations in the forest and dunes.

The triad-shaped Regenerative Virtues framework emerged during our first iteration of the Regenerative Capabilities framework, because we realised that there were some things that we didn't really know how to include in that Regenerative Capabilities framework but that, nevertheless, felt really important. Things that felt as if they were of a different order. Mieke – of the three of us most experienced with the various systemic frameworks developed by the Regenesis Institute – quickly realised that these 'things' perhaps required another framework, and that an 'energy setting triad' was likely the best option. That's how we started crafting the triad-shaped Regenerative Virtues framework, which we then also drew in the sand and developed in a similar manner to the capabilities framework.

Regenerative Paths – Journeying the Landscape of Regeneration

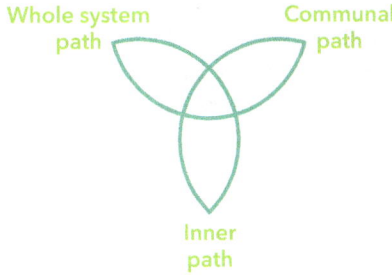

Figure 6: The Regenerative Paths framework.

By now, we've mentioned several times that regenerative educatorship is as much a journey inward as it is a process of reconnecting with your education peers and transforming education practices and structures. If your idea is to simply implement a curricular innovation and be done with it, we're going to have to disappoint you. It's not that easy. To truly face the complex questions of our times and co-create more life-affirming education potentialities, a whole lot more is needed. There is, to start with, an inner path to walk (see figure 6 above). A path of consciousness, of humbly opening up to your deep interconnection with all that lives, of picking up your unique biography, of exploring and developing your own narrative as to the purpose of education and the nature of education processes, and your role therein. A path of developing courage and commitment, and of acknowledging the magnitude of what you do not yet know or are not yet capable of. A path of opening up a developmental space within yourself and of nurturing this space. A space where you radically acknowledge that to change education practices, we must dare to begin with ourselves. In many ways, writing this book has – for each of us – been a sustained way of walking our inner path, and much of the reflective questions and intermezzos in this book are aimed at encouraging you to take steps on your own inner path.

Yet what the stories throughout the chapters illustrate over and over again is that there is also a communal path to walk, because real change doesn't happen through the actions of one person alone. It's in doing things differently together that new practices and cultural shifts manifest. Whether it's in crafting a classroom culture and dynamic in which agency is shared among teacher and students as Koen explored in chapter 2, nurturing a radically open space for experimentation and co-learning among educators and education innovators as Mieke explored in chapter 3, or uniting as a team to make a stance for a particular change in institutional policy as Bas explored in chapter 4, it's in the work of intentional communities that new education potentialities come into being.

Now, before we move to our third path, let us take a moment to consider how these first two paths are deeply interwoven. For one, it is often the support of a community that enables or invites us to walk the inner path. We know this all too well from our own collaboration and being part of a larger Community of Practice Regenerative Education. A community can offer support. But a community can challenge and confront as well. For instance, in the three examples provided above, all three of us experienced that we were challenged, and had to learn, to truly open up to the voice and desires of others, and to not hang on to some picture of an ideal outcome in our minds. In other words, the inner path is far from isolated from the context and community we are part of. And, similarly, shaping an intentional community is in many ways about truly connecting with each other, about sharing our inner journeys with each other and – with these others – becoming part of a shared and systemic endeavour, an endeavour we're all committed to.

The third path is more structural in nature. It's in realizing that the way the education system works in all its institutional layers and practices – the control systems, the curricular requirements, the space and time dedicated to education, a school's more or less explicitly formulated worldview and pedagogical vision, and so forth – is calling forth certain education experiences rather than others. And if the learning experiences that are being called forth are different from what we have good reason to want, if they are life-constraining rather than life-affirming, we might want to try and change the system. Now, we want to highlight that, often, a great deal of regeneration can occur by just taking matters in your own hands in your day-to-day interaction with students and colleagues. We do not need a new system to wake up and think, 'Today I'll do things differently'. There is, indeed, such a thing as individual and collective agency (let's not fall back into black or white thinking!). Yet this third path is all about recognizing how structures have agency as well, and about paving the way for structural change. It's about creating new conditions so that life-affirming education no longer depends on individual educators mustering up the courage to wake up thinking 'Today I'll do things differently'. And it is about standing up against those conditions which are degenerative. As such, this path is often one we're walking for the long run – and, yes, as chapter 5 perhaps showed most tangibly, this path, too, cannot be walked without an often rather large amount of inner work and intentional community building and support.

So, dear reader, if you're ready and motivated to step into or deepen your regenerative educatorship, we hope that the Regenerative Paths framework can help you see the different layers of the work that you may have to do to fulfil your potential. But we also want to acknowledge, at this point, that we're all different. Some people dive deeper into themselves than others. Some are more inclined to focus on large-scale system change, whilst others flourish in the close vicinity of their intimate classroom. Such differences are there to cherish, and it's up to each of us to explore what it might mean to take that next step in our own unfolding education biographies.

Regenerative Virtues – Showing Up with Regenerative Intent

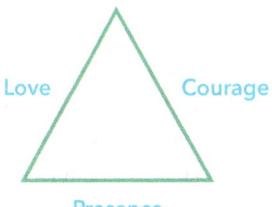

Figure 7: The Regenerative Virtues framework.

If you were to ask us what all the stories in this book of trying to work regeneratively within education systems radiate, or our shared journey of writing this book, for that matter, our answer would be this: love, presence, and courage (see figure 7 above). These are the three core virtues that make this work come alive, or at least they are the ones that do so for us. In our work with our peers in chapter 5, and in our conversations, workshops, and other experiences in the broader education field, we experience the same thing. Love, presence and courage are omnipresent in the success stories people tell, and in the frustrations and struggles they share there is a longing for them. Perhaps the virtues of love, presence, and courage provide an insight into what regenerative education experiences have in common, what their quality is. Let us explore each in some detail.

Love, we feel, is a powerful source for regenerative work. As we discussed in chapter 5 (as part of the fireplace conversation and in a footnote), our notion of love is a particular one, one that bears some resemblance to the notion of caring. It's about deeply recognising and appreciating the intrinsic value and potential of life, and longing for it to be fulfilled. In its highest form, this love is all-encompassing, it's an intrinsic commitment to a flourishing Earth, and the potential of all the life in it, now and into far futures. Yet in practice, it tends to be much more specific. It's something we tend to feel most strongly towards those we are closest to. It's perhaps more self-evident to approach one's own child as a unique being with intrinsic value than it is approach thirty students in a classroom in that way, let alone the many children yet to be born. Yet, this is what regenerative educatorship is inviting us into: to expand the scope of our love, to make it more integral, and to radiate it in all we do towards all we meet. Or, to frame it differently, it is to show up with love on all three

Regenerative Paths as explored above: to love ourselves, our colleagues and students, the institutes we are part of, and the larger human-made and natural systems they are embedded in. To love all of these things, including their, and our, many flaws. Now, it is very clear to us that experiencing and radiating love so integrally is a rare accomplishment, one that we ourselves have far from achieved, and one that probably is rather fleeting in the first place. It feels like a promise-beyond-ableness, but isn't that exactly what virtues are like? Something that we continuously strive for and rarely, and even then only momentarily, fully achieve.

To make it tangible how love – and, by extension, the other virtues as well – can be seen as a virtue to live up to across the inner, communal, and whole-system paths of regeneration, we would like to briefly revisit chapters 2 and 4. In chapter 2, Koen's story radiates a strong love for his students, whose existential questions and journeys he sought to create space for and support. Yet, he also confessed, at the end of the chapter, that he had not devoted as much energy to establishing connections with colleagues in his department or with questions of institutional change. Partially, Koen's experience is that this is due to self-protection, as focusing on a novel experiment with his students was already requiring a lot of energy and attention in itself and was what he felt a strong passion for at that time, a passion he didn't want to blur with the frustration of an overflowing plate and institutional hassle. Yet in all honesty, he also feels like he simply cared less – at that point in time – about his colleagues and institute than he did about his students. Now, we are not saying this particular orientation is good or bad. Yet, moving forward, Koen does wonder: 'What if I could radiate love for my colleagues and institute just as strongly? Would that radically change how I show up at work on a day-to-day basis?' This, to Koen, feels like a developmental potential. Now let's look briefly at chapter 4, where Bas's story radiates a strong belief in and commitment to the potential of his institute to evolve in a regenerative direction, as well as a strong love for the Earth more generally. Yet, he, too, confessed that at times he had not been caring enough towards his colleagues and their needs, nor towards himself and his own needs – that he had been so preoccupied with his institutional ideals and the worrying state of the natural world that he at times forgot to rest and be gentle to himself, and to approach his colleagues as unique human beings with their own stories, dreams, potentials, and developmental journeys. Just like Koen, Bas experienced this as a developmental potential, the potential to radiate love in all directions. Both Bas's story and Mieke's story about deeply caring for a community of peer educators illustrate that, sometimes, love means that we need to remain open to the possibility of letting go, or of hospicing parts of systems we care about. That is quite something to live up to. A lifelong quest, indeed. Interestingly, once Mieke came to terms with the idea that the FRIS community might come to an end, a new source of funding was found, and at the time of writing these last chapters, the community continues to exist and grow.

Whereas love is very much about how we approach the world, about how we feel and act towards others and ourselves, the second virtue – presence – draws attention to how we know and experience ourselves to be part of the world in the first place.

Presence is about being present, about standing firmly on the ground, about being in touch with the places we find ourselves part of, and with the others who live there, too. It is also about connecting with what is emerging all around us. It's about how we, from moment to moment, are open and attentive to the unfolding world around us, to what's really at stake in the places we are part of and for the beings we are entangled with. Or, as David Orr puts it, about being inhabitants rather than residents[3]. Yet presence is not only about being connected with the places, people, and other beings around us, but also about truly feeling inwardly, into ourselves – about being in touch with your body, your emotions, your needs, your intuition, your potential. And through all this, it is about standing firmly on the ground. If we are present to what presents itself in a particular place, in ourselves, and in the moment, it becomes much more possible and natural to approach life – as it unfolds – with a sense of calm, intention, and steadfastness[4]. It becomes much more possible, indeed, to love the world.

The virtue of presence is also clearly visible in the stories in this book and is a common thread throughout the fireplace conversation in chapter 5. To provide a few examples, it's visible in chapter 2 in how Koen invests time and energy in building a personal relationship with his students, through which he tries to get a sense of their process, and of what he might need to do to support it. It's visible in the deep commitment to co-creation that Mieke expresses in her story in chapter 4, and in her effort to create space for the voices of all her colleagues and in her protecting that space when particular colleagues become overbearing in it. It's in the work the three of us share to 'empty our minds' through activities like yoga, gardening, writing, surfing, Taichi, hiking, reiki, mountaineering, cooking, and meditating, helping us to be present in the moment. And just like with love, it's a virtue that's relevant across the inner, communal, and whole-system paths of regeneration. Analogous to what we just spoke about with respect to love, we tend to be more present easily in some contexts, places, or relationships than in others. This, too, is a lifelong practice. And quite a demanding one, we might add. For to be fully present, we need to be attentive time and again, inwardly and outwardly.

So, whereas presence is about truly being at home in ourselves and in the world and love is about the desire for all life to flourish and the inclination to serve this, courage is about taking action accordingly. And it takes courage to do so! A deep, impressive courage, whether it's about speaking with the board of your institute, who drafted a new strategic plan that you find profoundly missing in potential, about stepping into a co-creative space with students or colleagues in which you don't quite know where things are going, or about bringing your whole self – your life story, your quirks, your passions, your insecurities – more fully with you as you step into your role as an educator (note the Regenerative Paths in this sentence once more). Stepping into regenerative educatorship is often quite a stretch, involving doing things differently from what we're used to, or from what is valued by the system. It often feels vulnerable or disruptive. And perhaps it's exactly when it does so that we know we're doing work that matters.

Notably, sometimes the courageous thing to do is to actually stop doing something or to let something come to an end, to hospice. This, indeed, is an insight that runs through various of the earlier chapters of this book, and it is, interestingly, something Mieke is currently being with quite strongly as we're writing this chapter. Because, due to budget cuts which are rampant in Dutch education as we are finishing this book, the FRIS community, which she spoke of in depth in chapter 3, is under serious pressure, and she's wondering: What is the more regenerative thing to do here? Saving it at all costs or accepting that this is the end of this initiative and seeking ways to let it end well, with a beautiful harvest and plenty of seeds for new things to emerge or continue in other contexts? Opening oneself up to that second scenario does feel to Mieke as a rather confronting, vulnerable, and, indeed, courageous thing to do, for it means letting go of her identification with this project and stepping into an uncertain future. Yet – in this particular situation – it might just be the right thing to do. Or not? Perhaps you find yourself in a similar position. Imagine, if only it was always clear what the right thing to do is, right? Yet is not this ambiguity and uncertainty part of what makes courage so important? Doing what you're absolutely sure is the right thing to do but goes against business as usual can be hard and requires courage, but it requires plenty more courage to act when you yourself are doubting – which, after all, we so often are!

Now, one thing that has become very clear to us is that the stronger our sense of purpose, and the more connected we are, the more courageous and determined we tend to become. So, at least one way to look at the relationships among love, presence, and courage is this: Love is a source – it's what drives us to become educators in the first place – and a direction, giving us a sense of purpose. Presence connects us, makes us embedded in real, intimate relationships and contexts, provides us with a clear image of who we need to *be* and what it is we need to do in the name of love, and helps us to be steadfast in service of that love. Courage is the strong will and heart that enable us to do what needs to be done, even if it's scary and the outcome is uncertain. Love, presence, and courage – together – are a force to be reckoned with. Together they constitute an energy field within which regenerative projects can come to fruition. As such, they deserve to be cherished. The ongoing journey of keeping love, presence, and courage alive in yourself and in your communities is what we invite you into. We are sure that you already embody these virtues in numerous ways, perhaps unwittingly, perhaps purposefully. Yet we are also sure that – just as is the case for ourselves – taking a next step in developing your regenerative educatorship involves strengthening your relationship with these virtues across the inner, communal, and whole-system paths of regeneration. And we promise you, doing so is more than worth it, for what is more fulfilling than to be filled with a deep love, present through an open and attentive heart and mind, and empowered by the courage to make a difference that matters?

Regenerative Capabilities – Stepping into Regenerative Action

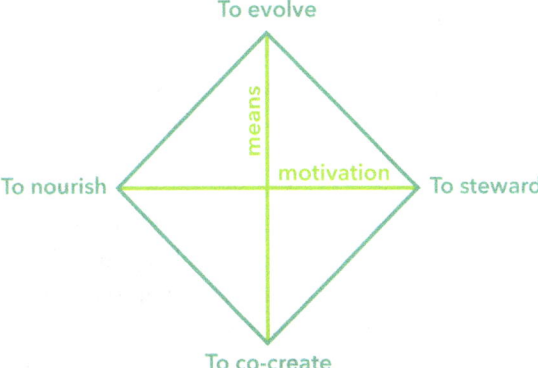

Figure 8: The Regenerative Capabilities framework.

If the Regenerative Virtues are about the energy field in which regenerative projects can flourish, the regenerative capabilities are about the more concrete practices along which regenerative projects take form (please see figure 8 above). They are our ability to shape these practices, to 'do the work' that this framework draws attention to. Of course, the work of regeneration is diverse, complex, and layered. Based on the first five chapters of this book alone, we could come up with a long list of different capabilities. Yet, we sense that the four capabilities which this framework dynamically brings together – the capabilities to nourish, steward, co-create, and evolve – integrate them quite well. Together, they tell a rich story of what it means to bring regenerative intentions into practice. So, let us take one last dive before we bring this chapter to a close.

We begin with the capability to nourish, on the left side of the framework. A clear pattern in the stories told and reflections shared throughout this book is that the effort to truly connect to people and place, and to listen to and invite their stories, plays a crucial part in processes of regeneration. What are the stories and the histories of your students, of their parents, of the diverse people in the neighbourhood, of your colleagues, of yourself, of the nature in your region, of the communities? What are the roots of your school, your institute, or your organization? Or, if there's frustration with a certain way things work, can you try to see how it came to be that way, what function it serves or once served, and how people are attached to it? And – as you do so – can you start to sense potential for development or regeneration? Can you sense a potential for things to change in a way that preserves or evolves the value that is also already there?

These are all questions related to the capability to nourish. But nourishing is not only about your effort to connect to the whole system as it is now – with all its regenerative and degenerative elements. It is also about trying to create spaces and settings in which this becomes a collaborative practice – and, crucially, about doing so in ways that create a deeper sense of community and that awaken a collective desire or motivation for regeneration. It lies in you inviting others to make their voices heard in your shared community. And in holding space for exploration, for the posing of questions, for listening to each other.

We've already explored how the Regenerative Paths and virtues are closely linked. Now let's briefly observe how the same goes for the capabilities. It is easy to see that the virtue of presence and the capability to nourish are related; when we want to nourish people or a place, our intention is to stand with them and to start seeing the potential to come more fully alive together. For this, we need to be open and receptive; we need to be present. The same goes for love: Holding space for others to explore and share their stories, to connect, is an act that reveals care, an act that is sourced in love. And, indeed, grounding your projects or initiatives in a sincere effort to open up to what's alive here and now is quite a courageous thing to do. In many ways it is much easier to just shape a project all by yourself based on your own private idea or objective than it is to subject your project to an ongoing search for what serves all involved. To ground your work like this, to open up like this, means that you're going to have to collaborate, that you might feel like you're losing control at times, that your own ideas and beliefs are going to be challenged, that you're stepping into an emergent space. That takes courage indeed.

Similarly, when we speak of the ability to nourish, the Regenerative Paths framework comes in handy. For, it might help us reflect on what or who it is that needs nourishing in a particular context or project. Perhaps it's you yourself whose voice needs to be supported and heard, perhaps your students, colleagues, communities. Perhaps the voice of your school or institute. Perhaps the voice of the land. Perhaps all of them. The stories we've developed in chapters 2, 3, and 4 each bear witness of a particular kind of nourishing. Koen, in chapter 2, appeared set on nourishing his students, by individually taking them on hour-long walks in the botanical gardens to get to know them, by inviting them to come up with a thesis topic that lies close to their heart, by inviting them to express themselves in a 'museum of our collective consciousness', and so forth. Mieke, in chapter 3, told a story full of the intention to nourish her colleagues, by not just offering innovation grants to educators, but by also inviting them into regenerative cafés, with check-ins in which she made sure everyone was provided the space to speak up and activities that were designed to strengthen each member's unique developmental journey and to learn with and from each other. Bas, in chapter 4, illustrated in numerous ways how he's been trying to open up space in institutional and political discourse for the voice of nature, and for the voice of students and colleagues who need or long for a profoundly different education experience. All these are examples of what we call the capability to nourish, and we can hardly imagine the regeneration of education practices without it.

If you move towards the capability to steward, you take a courageous, determined step into regenerative educatorship. For this is where you start noting that you have got something particular to do. In a way, it's where you start experiencing that you have been 'singled out'. For there is something that needs doing now that's lying on your plate, and not on someone else's. Of course, this doesn't emerge out of nowhere. It is when you experience a strong purpose – quite like the kind of love we spoke about before – are strongly connected to your context, and are fully conscious and present in the moment that you're likely to start experiencing this. Take, for instance, how Koen described, in chapter 2, how he strongly felt that he had to resist his student when they identified an option for shaping their thesis project around the installation of solar panels. It's through his nourishing – the relationship he'd built with this particular student, and the feel he had developed for the existential questions that they were living with – that he sensed that this particular choice would likely not serve their developmental journey as well as other possible choices could. Being driven by his pole star of – as formulated in chapter 2 – 'learning with a sense of belonging', he felt like he needed to do something in this particular moment in relation to this particular student. That's what stewardship is. It's when you experience that in a particular context your pole star requires you to act in a certain way, and to then muster the courage to do that. Just like how Bas reached a point together with others in his research centre – as he described in chapter 4 – when they felt it was appropriate to escalate in order to get proper attention for sustainability in the university's new strategic plan. Or how one of Mieke's first actions when she became coordinator of the FRIS project – as she described in chapter 3 – was to include the 'I' for inclusive. To steward, indeed, is to pick up the torch. To open yourself to the possible roles you can play in the ongoing regeneration of education practices. And to come more fully alive yourself in the process.

Together, the capabilities to nourish and steward describe a process of discovering the potential for regeneration in a particular context and developing the presence of mind and will to take responsibility for it in concrete situations. That's why their relationship – the horizontal line in the framework – carries the name 'motivation'. Yet, as you develop your regenerative educatorship, it's very likely that you will start to feel a motivation that is focused more on structural change. A motivation, to draw on chapters 2, 3, and 4 once more, to not just support this one particular student in this specific moment, but to develop a thesis community with a group of students to co-create an alternative track for the sustainability master's graduation year. Or a motivation, expressed by Bas in chapter 3, to reach out to all sorts of actors within the university to find an opening for institutionally embedding the possibility to graduate as a group. Or Mieke's motivation to shape FRIS as an active learning community across institutional borders with a strong sense of shared ownership. It's at this point, when we start to purposefully develop the means to support systemic change – i.e., the vertical axis in the framework – that we can really start to speak of regenerative projects, and that the capability to co-create becomes crucial.

Indeed, what we continue to experience is that if we want to make a durable, systemic difference, we need to build intentional communities and develop strategies that have a real chance of success. This, then, is where we find the somewhat naughty and playful guerrilla gardening we spoke of at length in chapter 3, the systemic acupuncture of chapter 4, and the constructive disruption with which we ended chapter 5. This is where the strategic and the playful come together. This is where all the nourishing and stewarding we step into in our day-to-day work enable us to identify synergetic projects, projects that bring together people around a shared purpose and that develop strategies that can effectively support the ongoing evolution of the whole system we are part of together. When we start focusing on this capability, it truly becomes impossible to avoid walking the inner, communal, and whole-system paths of regeneration in synchrony, because the kind of co-creation we speak of here is when multiple actors with similar desires to think and act differently (the inner path) start building intentional communities (the communal path) that develop projects aimed at systemic change (the whole-system path).

The Regenerative Virtues framework, too, continues to be of help here, for it invites us to truly explore, with open eyes and an open heart, the dynamic positions, needs, and developmental potential of different stakeholders and to make new, bold connections. It invites us to always stay connected to the source of love, to not get lost in a battle for power or a longing for acknowledgement, but to keep a bright image alive of the life-affirming education potential that makes this work worthwhile. And, to not dehumanize or instrumentalize our so-called adversaries or the restraining forces we encounter, but to see in them partners in a long-term evolutionary process. And it invites us to remain courageous, to be with the slowness and emergent character of the regenerative process, to do what we believe needs doing, and to simultaneously remain humble and continue to learn.

The Regenerative Virtues, in this way, actually help us to take yet one last step, the step into the capability to evolve. This capability comes into picture when we take a step back from the concrete regenerative projects we develop and try to see how, although they are perhaps really cool, they are part of a much larger process that spans across generations into the past and far into the future. Perhaps part of the art of regenerative educatorship is to not get too attached to your projects, to allow them to flow into the stream of evolution beyond your (all too human) tendency to control them. Some projects take off and turn out to be the start of something much bigger. Some don't. Yet even those that don't might be necessary steps in the bigger scheme of things. Much like how Mieke – in chapter 3 – described how FRIS was a project that came into being after several years of similar projects not taking off. Interestingly, as we mentioned before, at the moment of writing this chapter, it seems quite possible that FRIS is coming to an end itself. But if this is to be so, is this truly an end? After all, has FRIS not created ripples in various directions within the numerous departments of Mieke's university? Are the teachers who were part of FRIS not sustainably changed through their shared developmental journey? Did Mieke herself not grow in her own regenerative educatorship, and is she not ready now for a next step she couldn't have taken prior to FRIS?

In other words, in seeing ourselves as part of long evolutionary trajectories that are never contained in single projects, we can find the strength and deep purpose to continue to regenerate ourselves *and* our projects. To continue to wonder what's next, what else this journey of regenerative educatorship might have in store for you, and how you might step into roles you never imagined yourself capable of, in service of the larger system. The pole star of regenerative education – love for all life, truly life-affirming education systems and practices – is so bright that it can continue to inspire over and over again. Although the journey is full of surprises and can be as hard as it can be beautiful, isn't this a deeply reassuring thought? Sure, sometimes we may need to let go of a project or conclude it didn't go the way we had hoped. And sometimes we might find ourselves in a prolonged period of time in which everything seems to be getting worse. Yet at other times, things may take off beyond our expectations, and things we never held possible may come into being. Time will tell what fate is bestowed on FRIS. Perhaps it will continue in unexpected ways. Yet in any case, we're confident in saying that the true outcome of a project is usually far richer, and runs much further into the future, than what we tend to measure or count in project evaluations.

We hope that the Regenerative Capabilities framework, together with the Regenerative Virtues framework and the Regenerative Paths framework, can serve you. That they can help you shape and interpret your own journey and offer guidance when you're trying to figure out how to contribute to the regeneration of education systems and practices, or when you struggle to keep at it.

Notes

1. In chapter 4, this ecology of this constellation of elements is what Bas refers to as educational architecture.

2. We sense that the virtue of presence is gaining traction. It has intuitive links to notions like mindfulness and earthfulness, and perhaps it reminds you of the concept of 'presencing' that is used in Theory U (Scharmer, 2016). Fundamentally, this attention to presence can be considered part of a turn towards a relational worldview. The relational worldview – inherently part of living-systems thinking – holds that to live means to be deeply and intimately entangled with one's surroundings, and that there is no such thing as the truly separate individual. After all, there are many smaller organisms that live within us and without which we would not survive. And, similarly, the worldviews, ways of living, and experiences that we encounter as we are part of communities deeply shape how we make sense of life from moment to moment. And, reciprocally, our being in the world always touches the material and organic world we are part of. Perhaps the easiest way to be(come) aware of all this is to focus on the experience of breathing and to observe how the never-ending relationship you have with the very air around you literally binds you to this world, moves it, and makes you come alive. Many of the sources we highlighted throughout this book – such as the works of Daniel Wahl and Donna Haraway, to name but two authors – explore the depths and implications of relational worldviews, and how we've become detached from them in the modern western world. Also, we would like to mention Koen's doctoral dissertation here (2022), in which he explored in more detail how a relational worldview might inspire us to think differently about education relationships. Scharmer, C. O. (2016). *Theory U: Leading from the future as it emerges*. Berrett-Koehler Publishers. Wessels, K. R. (2022). *Pedagogy of entanglement: A response to the complex challenges of our time*. Springer.

3. Orr, D. (2013). Place and pedagogy. *The Namta Journal, 38*(1), 183–188. If we see ourselves as temporary residents of a place, we tend to just focus on our own immediate satisfaction and enjoyment, whereas if we truly become inhabitants, the place becomes part of who we are, and vice versa, and we develop a deeper attentiveness to what's going on in a place, as well as a sense of care and belonging.

4. Interestingly, we all have a strong connection with this notion through various embodied practices, like yoga, meditation, Taichi, and Judo. It has become very clear to us that such practices are an integral part not just of our personal lives, but of our work as regenerative educators, too.

Intermezzo
Working with Regenerative Frameworks

In the second section of this book, we transformed the implicit engagements with regenerative educatorship into explicit systemic frameworks: The Regenerative Paths framework, the Regenerative Virtues framework, and the Regenerative Capabilities framework. Their purpose is to systematically challenge how we think about our aims, experiences, and actions as education professionals, and to intentionally ground our practices and (change) projects in (more) regenerative modes of being, thinking, and acting. Another way of saying this is to frame these frameworks as (part of) a 'thinking technology' that invites a structured engagement with regeneration in your own context. We want to highlight, here, that this thinking technology extends beyond these three frameworks. In this book, we've made two other regenerative frameworks explicit, and both have played a large part in shaping this book and our thinking. These are the Levels of Work framework that we referred to in the introduction and the Law of Three framework that we referred to in chapter 3.

With this third and last intermezzo, we would like to invite you to actively work with these frameworks – to try them out for yourself, to see what they elicit. To support you in this endeavour, we would like to offer a bit more context as to how to work with regenerative frameworks, as well as a brief summary of the added value of the five presented in this book. In our experience, it works well to approach all this with a touch of playfulness and lightness. It's not about getting everything right; it's about opening up how we think and act as we move within education practices and systems. It's about collectively growing the regenerative current in education.

As a thinking technology, these frameworks can be worked with in three main ways. They can be worked with *retrospectively*, to gain a deeper understanding of how a previous project or experience unfolded, to start seeing what potential was and wasn't actualised, and to develop a sense of what was needed to actualize that potential more fully. They can be worked with *presently*, to develop a deeper and present understanding of the regenerative potential of an event/process you are currently in the middle of, and to support you in figuring out how to contribute to its unfolding on the go. And they can be worked with *prospectively*, to purposefully design regeneration into future events and projects. In all these instances, it can be valuable if you work with these frameworks individually, but it tends to become more transformative for all involved if you use them to design (implicitly or explicitly) how you learn and work together as a team or community. This way, regenerative thinking becomes built into the process of team/community development.

We have been holding these frameworks in mind while working on our own education projects and experiences for a while now, and it's our experience that doing so becomes increasingly intuitive as the frameworks become more and more internalised and you start developing your own sense of how each framework is valuable and when. Figure 9 provides a visual representation of each of the frameworks in this book, complemented by a brief summary of their added values and a set of questions that might support your active engagement with them:

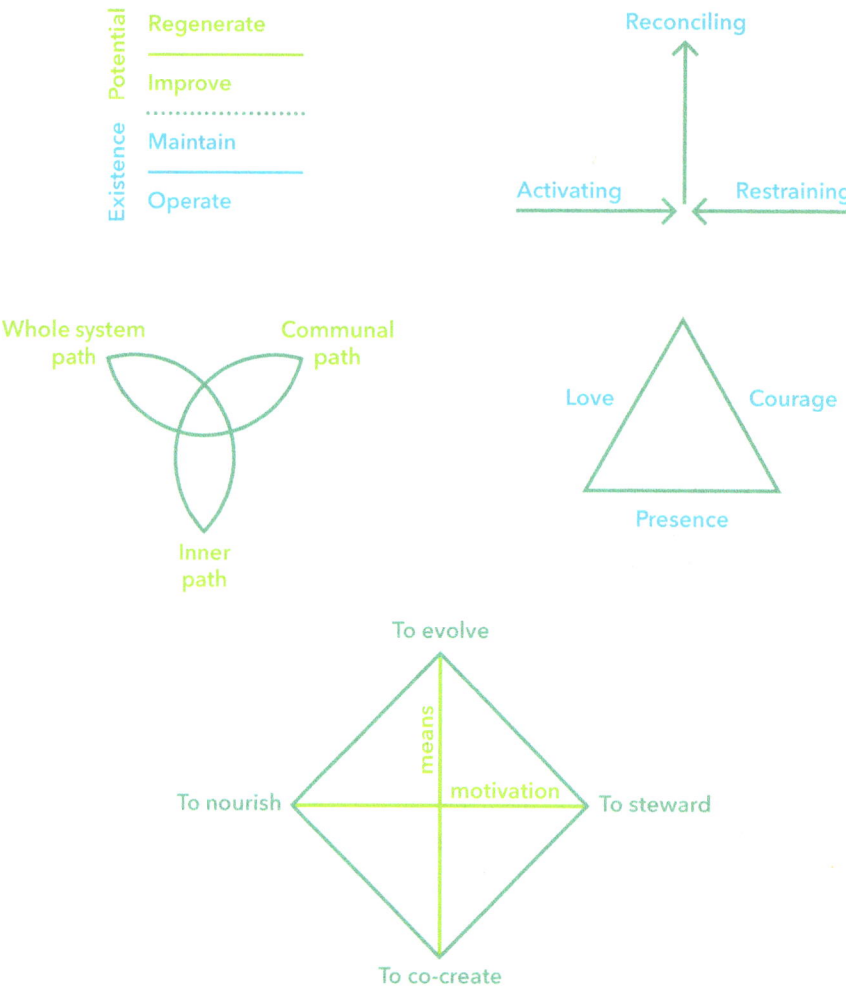

Figure 9: The regenerative frameworks in this book. Top left: Levels of Work; top right: Law of Three; middle left: Regenerative Paths; middle right: Regenerative Virtues; bottom: Regenerative Capabilities.

- The Levels of Work framework offers a powerful entry point into regenerative thinking and working, as it invites you to explore to what extent you're spending your time and energy reactively – solving problems, often in isolation, that arise from within 'business as usual' – and to what extent you manage to elevate your thinking to a systemic level of seeing patterns and imaging potential for evolution for the whole systems you work with. *Can you recognize on what levels you are working currently, and/or habitually? And what would it entail to shift from working on the levels of existence to working on the levels of potential? And, how can you harmonize these different levels and appreciate the value of each of them in the bigger scheme of things?*

- The Law of Three framework reminds us that regenerative processes are never straightforward implementations of ideas or initiatives. Rather there's always a mix of activating, restraining, and reconciling forces, and it is in our capacity to see how all are necessary for the evolution of systems – especially when we start seeing possible paths of reconciliation. This leads to an increase in vitality and viability of a system as a whole, rather than polarisation and fragmentation. *What are the activating and restraining forces in your context? How are you and your co-creators/students/colleagues/stakeholder currently working with these forces? What would it mean to embrace both together and commit to finding reconciling paths that serve the evolution of the larger whole? Can you see such reconciling paths and the potential they work towards?*

- The Regenerative Paths framework invites us to explore how layered processes of regeneration are, as they always involve interconnected processes of inner development, community building, and system evolution. This framework supports us to keep seeing this wholeness, to question what each path asks from us, and how the paths can be(come) aligned with each other in developmental ways. *Which paths are you currently walking, and how? Would you say there's a path you're neglecting? What would it mean to bring them in alignment? Are you able to articulate 'what you're called to do' on each of them? And what can resource you in your process of stepping into and being steadfast in these roles?*

- The Regenerative Virtues framework invites us to be(come) grounded in the spirit or energy of regenerative projects: A deep experience of love for all life, which can form the heart of and basis for everything we do. A profound presence in and with the systems and places we are part of and all the life that co-exists within it, which enables us to sense potential and forms the basis for developing projects that truly matter. And a steadfast courage, a strong will and heart that enable us to keep developing ourselves and our work no matter how dire the situation or how uncertain the outcomes. Of all the frameworks we share here, perhaps it is the Regenerative Virtues that is most suited to serve as a compass. It tends to gently yet relentlessly invite you to keep walking a regenerative path. *Can you observe, from moment to moment, if your actions are grounded in love, presence, and courage? What are your own inner obstacles to loving, to be present, and to be courageous, and can you actively choose how you want to show up in the moment? What can resource you in this process? And how can you help create a collective energy field that invites you and your community to be loving, present, and courageous together?*

- The Regenerative Capabilities framework is perhaps the most practical of the frameworks shared here, as it invites you to systematically think about how you shape regenerative projects. It invites you to nourish the nested stories of individual people, (education) communities, education programs and systems, and the wider context or place in which they are embedded. What are these stories of people and place in your context? Tapping into the dynamic relationships between these stories, what wants to become more fully alive here? What *developmental potential do you sense?* As you work with these questions, it's quite natural to move to the right side of the framework. *What can you – with your own story, unique potential, and roles – do to become aligned with the unfolding of potential? Who are you called to be(come) here, what are you called to do (e.g. protect, resist, initiate, disrupt ...), and how can you grow your capacities to do so?* This framework also reminds us that to truly work on a systems level, we need to co-create. *Who are the different actors or stakeholders who are or could become invested in the regenerative potential you, too, are working on? How could your efforts and activities coalesce? And what does it ask of you to truly step into a co-creative space?* And, last, this framework invites us to keep practicing a sense of openness, humility, and adaptability as our projects evolve and weave into the evolutionary processes of the systems and communities we're working with. *How can you keep those questions around nourishing, stewarding, and co-creating alive rather than treating them instrumentally? Can you see how your projects are part of processes of a much longer timespan and how they touch your and others' lives in ways beyond immediate project goals? Are there things it's time to let go of, so that energy can flow to what wants to begin anew, and evolve?*

7 Closing Words: Gratefulness and Recommitments

We opened this book by writing individual opening statements; we close this book by writing letters. This time, our invitation is shaped and inspired by our collective action of nurturing this book into existence, as well as by our life journeys and professional pathways as they became increasingly entangled over many weekends, trips, and even a transcontinental wedding. Once you read the epilogue, it will become clear to you that this entanglement is likely to escalate further (we have come to embrace the notion of 'existendipilation', as we framed it in the introduction). For, in parallel with completing this book, we have started co-creating a School of Regenerative Educators. We hope that this book has been as transformative for you to read as it has been for us to co-create. We also know that it will likely take many more months and years for all the rippling of this book to manifest itself in our own engagement with regenerative educatorship. We hope that it works in a similar way for you. In each of our closing letters, we reflect on how this endeavour has been transformative for ourselves and, perhaps most importantly, what new 'long-thought' question(s)[1] it encourages us to hold. In a way, by sharing all this with you, we hope to inspire you to develop your own unique long-thought question. Or, in the words of our mentors at Regenesis Institute, to help you gain a deeper understanding of your promise-beyond-ableness as a regenerative educator.

Letter by Mieke

Dear reader, regenerative educator, friend,

I am developing this closing letter for our book as I walk through Bergen, during the last few hours of one of the various writing retreats that helped manifest this book. I am walking through a field of grass and trees, and the air is a bit cool, cooler than yesterday during our sunny forest walk. I am recording my thoughts, which I am speaking out loud, to be transcribed and refined later. It feels natural to voice-record my thinking, as this is directly inspired by our collective ways of imaging – and quite literally walking-our-talks – as we recorded our framework-focused conversations over the past few days (which formed chapter 6). And, speaking out loud also brings a sensation of making things real, speaking out loud honestly, openly – even when a soft inner voice in my mind questions if I really dare to be so open and vulnerable. Catching myself thinking this, as happens so often, I again invite myself to remember to source my thinking in the virtues of love, presence, and courage. Regenerating my thinking is truly a daily, moment-to-moment practice and commitment.

I can tell from the slight itch in my stomach that it does really take courage to speak out loud and express my heart-felt reflections to you in this book. And I think I can only do so because of being connected to the collective energy field Bas, Koen, and I built and nourished as we worked together. It's quite a powerful and nourishing field to be a part of – and one which I hope we extend to you, our dear reader, as you engage with this book and the Regenerative Virtues framework. So that together, we practise and develop our capabilities to speak openly from love, presence, and courage to ourselves internally; to speak and connect in solidarity and from care about those we work with; and to muster the courage to speak up against parts of the systems and societies we are embedded within that require transgressions and hospicing.

Being part of this book journey has been quite an adventure. I notice it is not easy to capture the full extent of the meaning of this developmental journey that I experienced personally. Little did I know … that 'writing a book together' would bring about a quality of 'existendipilation'; that it would foster friendship; and that Bas, Koen, and I would support each other through dark times and celebrate moments of incredible joy together. And that we would, together, find enormous support and encouragement from the members of the Community of Practice Regenerative Education, from our resources, mentors, friends, and family around us. And that from all this, the idea of a 'school' would start to emerge. I can truly say that I feel a deep sense of gratitude and a warm heart for having been able to walk this adventurous, joyful, challenging, disruptive, and transgressive path together so far, and for living with the prospective of strengthening the regenerative current in education, together with a growing community, for a long time to come.

And as I say these words, a lively image emerges of the journey of this book and how it evolved into a living being itself – enriched by the multiple road trips, various walks in nature, and shared meals – oftentimes lovingly prepared by Bas or Sofia. How stepping into Koen's bright yellow car at Utrecht Centraal station – with Bas gallantly squeezing in the back so I can sit next to Koen in the front and won't get car sick (thank you) – is without exception the start of another, often unexpected, deep dive into the various stories and sections which made this book. The image of a living book has been our pole star as we developed this work together, navigating (with a little help of online navigation systems) to different parts of the Netherlands, Belgium, and even Türkiye, celebrating Koen's wedding. Other parts of the book were developed in contexts including Norway, Mexico, Spain, and the United States through our individual travels and dedicated writing time while we were away. While the emergence of the Community of Practice that sourced this living book, and of the School of Regenerative Educators, has its roots in the watery and fertile soil of the Netherlands, its arms and legs, thoughts and dreams, and unfolding adventures reach into different parts of the globe, connected to different places and being resourced in different regenerative and developmental communities.

The painting of the aliveness and being quality of this book was further coloured in through the experience of an organisational constellation workshop we took part in, to work on the development of the School of Regenerative Educators. I was truly amazed by the power of having a group of participants literally embody various key elements of the question we brought with us: of how the School of Regenerative Educators was unfolding in relation to its nested systems and stakeholders, with this book being a catalyst. We witnessed this book being represented by a woman who before that date never heard of us, the school, or regeneration, let alone regenerative education. I recall how impressed I felt that the book has become the energetic expression of so much enthusiasm, curiosity, joy, and adventurousness – as a living entity so full of energy. And it was also really humbling to then see how the person representing this book - as a 'living entity' in the constellation - related itself with deep respect to the various communities it is connected to, to our lineage of our mentors, and to our resources connected to the Regenesis Institute. How a very tall man representing higher education very slowly started to show some interest in and curiosity towards this work. And how this book is only a small stepping stone, forming part of a much larger field of endeavour, with the School of Regenerative Educators organically, perhaps unstoppably, manifesting out of it. I remember how I felt a sense of caring and deep responsibility when I witnessed another female participant representing the School of Regenerative Educators, and how her steadfastness, calmness, serenity, wisdom, silence, and groundedness made a lasting imprint on me. So while Bas, Koen, and I, full of curiosity, jumped into this book project, I think we are now stepping with much more consciousness and dedication into the next phases of our collectively unfolding journey through the School of Regenerative Educators.

In a way, the journey of co-developing this living book together often felt like what in yoga philosophy would be called a *sukha*, or easeful way of working. And while opening up to new levels of reflexivity, honesty, vulnerability, and openness required a great sense of courage and trust, it has never felt stressful or forced. I am pretty sure I would not have been able to take these leaps of faith without the loving support of Koen and Bas. Thank you, for jokingly forcing me to stop saying sorry so often, and to find more courage, more depth of understanding, and increasing faith in speaking and standing up for more regenerative and connected ways of being and learning together – which is a daily act of resistance and courage when you are working in an overheated, fast-paced, and highly individualised and polarised university, school, or societal context. Just like I've done during my decades-long daily discipline of a reiki self-treatment, I will need to continue to work on a daily commitment and discipline to remind myself of truly living the three Regenerative Virtues of love, presence, and courage. Regenerative work and educatorship for me finds resonance with the inspiration I find in the reiki principles I learned from my reiki masters Rebecca Bredenhof and Corien van Vliet, which I try to live by as a daily practice:

Just for today, do not worry
Just for today, do not anger
Honour your parents, teachers and elders,
Earn your living honestly
Show gratitude to every living thing

When I am in need of courage, and faced with challenging moments or invitations which feel scary in the field of (higher) education – or, more broadly, in my other roles in life – I am practicing to call upon the courage of my ancestors, the loving wisdom and consciousness of my teachers, the resourcing support of the reiki resource development community in the Netherlands, and the presencing quality my children are showing me -- and in the midst of today's pressures, polarisation, and overheated systems, to aim to show up with a being quality grounded in these virtues. It is no easy task.

It is my true hope that through sharing our stories and explorations, and through engaging in regenerative framework thinking, that we invite you to (continue to) explore your own unique regenerative educatorship. If you have made it to this last part of the book, then I foresee a likelihood that our paths will cross so that we can (un)learn together what regenerative educatorship is about. I sincerely hope that this book becomes a resource for further connectivity and for community building in a truly developmental, regenerative way. It's also what I'm ready to commit to, to step into, to hold, to nourish, to resource. It is my promise-beyond-ableness that I wish to make as I close this letter, connecting to the long-thought question of the regenerative potential of our learning systems or education systems that we've developed as humanity in order to become loving, present, courageous, creative, and caring human beings. And together explore how to breathe more life, more vitality, more viability, more evolutionary potential into learning systems, by jointly working on our inner beings and our inner transformations as regenerative educators, and in doing so, serve and transform the learning potential of the learning living systems – and living learning systems – around us. *Caminando*, walking this path together, *hacia el sol*.[2]

With love, presence, and courage,
Mieke

Letter by Bas

Dear reader, regenerative educator, friend,

Strangely enough, it feels bittersweet to be writing this final letter. I am writing while sitting on a beach, facing the North Sea. Sitting here, the day before my birthday and just after returning from a writing retreat for this book, amongst the forests and dunes of the north of the Netherlands, I am listening to the waves gently breaking on these sandy beaches. I am enjoying the bittersweetness of the inbetweenness that I experience as I go about crafting these final words. The bitterness of this moment is the death of this collective writing process, yet that is amply compensated for by the sweetness of sharing this work with you and with the world. You may imagine this was an exciting moment. I hope that this work helps you to re-engage with your own journeys as you engage (further) with regenerative educatorship. I cannot do much more beyond speculate what the ripples of this work might be. I can, however, sit here in silent reflection and listen to the waves. Listen to the movements that are rippling. If you, dear reader, have made it this far with us, perhaps I can invite you to do the same. To find some water and listen to it for a moment more. Working on this project has been regenerative for myself. It has, indeed, been healing for my inner path. Working on this book together has in many ways acted as a lifeline when I was in the dark depths of fighting dragons[3], when there was plenty a moment where I struggled with being in the depths, being numb, and even suicidal – not living fully the kind of hope that we espouse in this work and our very being. Or perhaps, not daring to fully live into it. I think it is fair to say that I was shaken in my ability to be present. It does indeed take quite a bit of courage to stay steadfast when you are facing such a mighty adversary as dragons.

One of the community of practice members who helped co-create chapter 5 mentioned how I can be unyielding in my regenerative commitments. And how it may not always be easy for those around me when my steadfastness challenges existing practices. I would like to thank Mieke and Koen for allowing me to be unyielding with them. I hope that you, dear reader, find your tribe where you get to be unyielding too. The capabilities that Koen and Mieke showed me in regard to allowing me to be vulnerable are part of their expressions of love towards the potential of education spaces. I hope to one day live up to their examples. Perhaps, our explorations of the inner landscapes we inhabit act as a gentle invitation for you to do the same. This work has illuminated in many ways how I wish to show up in the world. How I can be more loving, courageous, and present in my education path. It has helped to resource me when my own ambitions exceeded the potential-beyond-ableness of the university I was working with(in). I am sure that you will encounter similar struggles. I hope that our work has provided you with ways of navigating these frustrations. Perhaps you may have even found ways in which you can actively hospice, within yourself, your community or system, as part of your regenerative educatorship.

I know there will be more bouts with the dragons of my life, as the poet Rilke would say. That is one of the many gifts you receive when you live with a chronic illness. Nor do I imagine that we will be able to quickly heal the education system from the many degenerative elements that it currently harbours. Indeed, the education system is also full of dragons - large behemoths that act as restraining forces and, potentially, wise teachers if we are courageous to engage with them. I hope this work may help you see some of these dragons and engage with them more effectively. Indeed, my deepest hope for this work is that it may be a resource that you, our dear reader, may pick up in different moments when it is most needed. So, I hope that together we have crafted a guide that allows you, in a way, to recentre, recharge, reconnect, and recalibrate for the next leg of your adventure into regenerative educatorship. A helpful resource for those moments in your education artistry when you notice it becomes hard to truly embody love, presence, and courage for the regenerative potential all around us. For if you are like me, I know you will experience such moments. I wish for you all to find partners like I did in Mieke and Koen. People who help you to show up with love, courage, and presence. People who revitalise and challenge your response-ability. People who dare to ask if you are truly stepping into your regenerative educatorship. I would be lying if I said that I never considered leaving academia, or even education. Perhaps you have the same doubts at times. I hope that the potential that we tried to show in this work may give you strength in those moments. Because where else in society can you find the potential to truly focus on developing human potential to foster healthier realities? There is a great privilege in being able to work in education - to play an active part in the welcoming into the world of the generations that come after us. At the very beginning of this book, we mentioned a quote from Daniel Wahl that one of the best gifts you can give are better questions to live. I hope that we have been able to help you find better questions to live.

With love, presence, and courage,
Bas

Letter by Koen

Dear reader, regenerative educator, friend,

Today - 11 September 2024 - I've sat myself down in the public library of Utrecht to write my closing words for this book. I've been delaying doing so, and I know why. It's not because I don't want this writing journey to end. This whole book project has evolved in such a way that I know this is just a beginning. No, it's more that I've been waiting for the moment that I felt enough clarity to speak about how the writing of this book took place during quite a turbulent phase of my life, and what this has made me realise with regard to some of the central themes of this book.

One part of this 'turbulence' is that at the beginning of 2024, I left a 4-year postdoctoral research contract at Utrecht University halfway through. This decision came after quite an intense period of trying my best to make the project I had been committed to a success in the experience of everyone involved. Yet in doing so, I had slowly come to realise that the project had evolved in such a way that I no longer felt like I belonged to it. That the direction in which the project was evolving felt too far removed from regenerative educatorship. And that it asked of me to step into a role that alienated me from myself, and that it felt like it did not invite or enable me to live up to my potential to add value from within a higher education institute. I felt like the moment had come to hand over the torch to someone who'd feel like this particular project was created for them, and to open space for myself to redirect my energy. More generally, I experienced, not for the first time in my life, that 'slowing down and taking a breath' and 'following the impulses of one's heart' are rather hard things to do in our overly cognitive, overheated, and competitive (higher) education system. A system, indeed, that I often experience as reactive rather than intentional, and which I'm afraid does more harm than we like to admit. Also, I've come to see that the times in my life in which I was best able to add value to education systems were those times during which I dared to walk an unconventional path, be it within or outside of institutional settings - like my work with Mieke and Bas.

The reason I wanted to share this in this closing letter is that it relates directly to the question of belonging, with which I started my opening statement to this book and which runs through this book as a common thread. It's become increasingly clear to me that belonging - for instance to a job, to a project, or, more broadly, to an education system - is a journey that's never finished. Nor is it always easy. It can be hard work, it can be confrontational, and it can come with lots of insecurity. One of the things that makes it hard - at least in my experience - is the voice of ambition, which can blur our vision. After all, publishing papers and climbing the academic ladder - my version of 'the conventional path' - comes with status, boosts one's ego, and is widely admired in our society. And then there's fear of failure. Speaking for myself, I have to admit that the whole idea of a fixed contract at a university, with all the security and stability it provides, is wildly attractive. Or perhaps a more accurate way to put it would be: It's wildly attractive to the little child in me, who used to have nightmares and irrational fears about ending up 'in the gutter'. My work on this book with Mieke and Bas, and the emphasis on potential that is so deeply anchored in regenerative thinking, has helped me tremendously in embracing these parts of myself and somewhat letting go of their grip on me. My own ongoing journey of grounding myself in the virtues of love, presence, and courage - this is very clear to me - plays a crucial role here. This, in turn, enables me to really dare ask: If I take the notions of regeneration, of belonging, of potential seriously, and if I want to continue to evolve my own capacity to serve the regeneration of education systems, what decisions do I have to make? What should I move towards, and what should I leave behind? How, in other words, am I to dance with the system? I am forever grateful for the effects that working on this book have had on me, and my biggest dream for this book is that it can have a similar effect for you. All in all, I've come to experience a strong faith in the power of regenerative thinking to aid all of us in this process of building trust, courage, and will.

The other 'turbulent thing' I wanted to share is that I had a rather severe car accident just as I was about to leave Utrecht University. At the end of January 2024, my partner and I were visiting friends in Kars, in northeastern Türkiye. It was super snowy, and on the way to visit an archaeological site, an approaching car veered into our lane and we had a head-on collision at around 70 km/h. This is the kind of accident that is potentially fatal, and it feels like a small miracle that we're all doing well today. So, as it happened, I spent the entire first month after leaving Utrecht University fully dedicated to recovering from this crash, both physically and psychologically. In hindsight, the way this forced me to come to an absolute standstill may have been of value (not that I advise it). It's interesting how such experiences can make us aware of just how much time and energy we spend on things we don't really care about or believe in. And what an immense waste it is when the potential of human beings to thrive in mutuality with the places and communities they are part of remains unfulfilled, as it often does. It's also made me experience firsthand how resilient the human body and spirit actually are. This is an experience I draw hope from. I think we're stronger than we often give ourselves credit for, both individually and collectively. Speaking for myself, it's been heartwarming to be supported by Mieke and Bas through this experience, and to feel – in my whole being - that our work on regenerative education is truly making me come alive.

So, yeah, my closing words are that I am deeply grateful for the journey this book has become, and that I hope it can be of service to you and the systems you move within. For me, this collective plunge into regenerative ways of thinking and acting has made all the difference, and I am truly excited for the journey that lies ahead. At the centre of this book has been the notion of regenerative educatorship. But working on it has given me a taste, more broadly, of what it means to live a regenerative life. I cannot promise you that I won't at times worry too much, get stuck into a problem-solving mindset, or alienate myself from the world. But the well of love runs so deeply, and I sense so much regenerative education potential, that it makes my chest burst with joy and energy. We've all got a role to play, and I can't wait to play it together!

With love, presence, and courage,
Koen

Notes

1. See Sanford, C., & Haggard, B. (2023). *No more gold stars*. InterOctive.
2. Referring to the song *Caminando* by Rising Appalachia: https://www.risingappalachia.com/
3. Bas wrote a novel called *De draken in mij* (*tr*. The dragons inside me), a fictionalised account of living with and being with chronic pain as represented by what Rilke refers to as the dragons of our lives. The novel is the first of a trilogy about *acceptance* (April 2025), *resilience* (October 2025), and *steadfastness* (date t.b.d., 2026).

Epilogue
The School of Regenerative Educators

During the work on this book, it became clear for us that just writing it was not enough. We started to sense a deeper potential, purpose and will. We felt like the Earth, and the education systems we are part of, asked us to step up our game, so to speak. This, lovingly and continuously, escalated into the formation of the School of Regenerative Educators. This is an organization launched in 2024 by the three of us with the purpose of nurturing the regenerative current in education. The school nourishes several offerings for educators who wish to further unleash and develop their own potential to contribute to more regenerative education systems and practices. Among these are an online developmental learning community and intensives for collective deep-dives. In addition, if you feel the call to work on regenerating your education space, place, and/or teams we would be honoured to develop dedicated resourcing opportunities for this. So, now that this book has manifested, the school is further along its journey of becoming.

As this book has hopefully made clear, the three of us are all deeply affected by the further break down of our planet. And it hurts us to see the disconnection so many human beings experience from themselves, each other, and nature. We sense so much unfulfilled potential, so much opportunity to live lives of harmony and co-evolution. We share the deep belief that education can be a greatly emancipatory force not just for humans, but for all life. With the School of Regenerative Educators, we hope to nurture that potential. You can find more information about the school and the possibility of working with us by visiting www.regenerative-educators.com or by emailing school@regenerative-educators.com. We hope to see you there.

So, there it is. The end of this book. If you have been touched by the regenerative potential of education like we have been, it will be clear to you that the regenerative current in education is urgent, and that it is growing. Let's surf those waves together!

Thank you for reading, and thank you for taking the time to engage with regenerative educatorship.

Bas, Koen, and Mieke

Dedications and Acknowledgements

This work would not have been possible without the love and support of many. Each of us is intimately connected to communities and individuals all around us. While it is impossible to thank them all for their love, we will do our best. Firstly, we would like to thank those closest to us: Rikjan, Ramses and Samin, Astrid, Gizem, and Papyon. They are pillars in our lives, and we are eternally grateful for their patience and energy, which have allowed us to do this. We are also thankful to our parents, siblings, and other beloved family members (human or otherwise) who have each helped to resource us in their own ways. Of course, we could not have done it without the loving friendships that each of us has in our life. Thank you all. This book is dedicated to you, and to our collective love for our communities and the Earth.

Secondly, we are grateful to the organisations that have housed and supported us and the work that we do, including the department of Geography, Planning and International Development Studies at the University of Amsterdam and The Centre of Expertise Mission Zero at The Hague University of Applied Sciences. We kindly thank the supportive colleagues, editors and designers at Amsterdam University Press and the Institute of Interdisciplinary Studies for taking the intellectual risk of taking on this topic and for helping us successfully move this project to publication.

A deep bow to our students, our key stakeholders in our journeys as regeneratively aspiring educators. You continue to inspire us to evolve our work and, indeed, ourselves.

We would like to acknowledge the importance of having supportive colleagues around us, and thank colleagues in the Governance and Inclusive Development research group, the International Development Studies programme at the University of Amsterdam (UvA): thank you especially Michaela Hordijk, Maggi Leung, Courtney Vegelin, Esther Miedema, Hebe Verrest, Yves van Leynseele, Joyeeta Gupta, Mirjam Ros-Tonen, Line Kuppens, Joeri Scholten, Karen Paiva-Henrique, S. Shakti, Crelis Rammelt, Elizabeth Kruger and other dear colleagues for your support and willingness to engage in regenerative explorations. We are also grateful for the support to the FRIS community, spcially from Mariska Min-Leliveld at UvA's Teaching and Learning Centre, Linda de Greef at the UvA Institute for Interdisciplinary Studies, and Machiel Keestra at the Chief Diversity Office.

We kindly thank Mission Zero for providing the funding for the open access fees of this book, as well as the years of support and nurturing that have allowed the regenerative education field to further develop. Thank you all, especially Jolanda Lutteke, Sander Mertens, Anja Overdiek, Kim Poldner Baldiri Salcedo, Rizal Sebastian, and Liliya Terzieva.

We are also grateful to our mentors and guides, some of whom you have met in this book, many of whom have lived through it. A few of them participated directly in the resourcing of earlier drafts of this text or as patient listeners when we were stuck. We would like to explicitly thank Luca Bertolini, Rolien Blanken, Daan Buijs, Wouter Buursma, Sidney Cano, Jonas Carinhas, Aniek Draaisma, Debby Gerritsen, Ben Haggard, Ingeborg Heezen, Anthony Heidweiller, Michaela Hordijk, Alette Los, George Lengkeek, Pamela Mang, Josine Pennings, Sidsel Petersen, Nuno da Silva, Marlies van der Wee-Bedeker, Tom de Wit, and Phyllis Wong for providing us with encouraging and insightful reflections on their experience of reading drafts of this book, which helped us tremendously.

We kindly thank the Community of Practice Regenerative Education for their contributions to this work, and for being the place where the seed for this book was planted. We are grateful for the many years of resourcing support and collective learning facilitated by Ben Haggard and Rebecca Bredenhof in the Regenerative Resource group of reiki practitioners which Mieke is a part of: a deep bow to Ingrid van Alst, Anne Boerrigter, Annemarie Karsten, Robert Kramps, Josine Pennings and Mirjam Top-ter Maat. We also kindly thank the Regenesis Institute and broader regenerative community for all of their (in)direct contributions, and specifically Nicholas Mang for resourcing us in the process of developing this 'living book' and in the emergence of the SRE. We are grateful for the teachings and inspirations of Carol Sanford, who, sadly, passed away during the last months of writing this book, and who leaves a rich fount of wisdom which will undoubtedly continue to resource our endeavours moving forwards. We are thankful for the contributions to the field and our thinking made by Daniel Christian Wahl. We thank Pamela Mang for generously sharing her wisdom and for her encouragement of our work. Our gratitude goes to Ben Haggard, for being an incredibly generous and committed mentor and resource in this work for so many people and systems, and for radically impacting on the course of our own lives in regenerative ways.

Finally, we thank you, dear reader, for your curiosity, courage, and openness to engage in this shared learning journey, and we hope our currents of life will meet.

About the Authors and Co-creators

Mieke Lopes Cardozo currently serves as associate professor in Regenerative Education and Development in the International Development Studies programme and the Governance and Inclusive Development Research Group of the University of Amsterdam. She lives in Amsterdam with her partner and is a devoted mother of twins, a committed reiki practitioner and yoga teacher, a member of the Regenerative Resource Development Community in The Hague. She is co-founder and co-director of the School of Regenerative Educators.

Bas van den Berg currently serves as associate professor in regenerative leadership at the Centre of Expertise Mission Zero of The Hague University of Applied Sciences, where he also serves as member of the management team of the Masters in Sustainability Transitions in the faculty of Business, Finance and Marketing. He lives in Dordrecht with his partner, is a fervent player of (video) games including Dungeons & Dragons and writes novels. He is co-founder and co-director of the School of Regenerative Educators.

Koen Wessels currently serves as a regenerative educator at the University of Amsterdam. He's a core lecturer on 'change making' within the Computational Social Sciences bachelor programme and serves as a resource and trainer for the Interdisciplinary Social Sciences teacher community. He lives in Utrecht with his partner and his canine companion. Through his partner, he has rooted himself in a second culture and country – Türkiye – and developed a deep passion for the transformative potential of intercultural experiences. He is co-founder and co-director of the School of Regenerative Educators.

Sofia Sarmienta Aboleda served as a resource during the co-creation process of this book. She did so initially as a student assistant and later as a dear friend. She is currently living a nomadic lifestyle with her life partner, Dart, and their dog, Naima, travelling across Europe and the world.

Nicholas Mang serves as developmental editor for this book and the emergence of the School of Regenerative Educators. In this role, he helped slow us down and stretch our thinking when required. He currently serves as one of the core faculty for the Regenesis Institute, including for its Regenerative Practitioner (TRP) and Storying Place series of offerings.

Testimonials

"This book is a timely provocation to all of us to consider being a regenerative educator as an important role that we can develop as an art form. Since regeneration is inherently developmental from the cellular to the ecosystemic to human learning, we all can become better regenerative educators for each other as we continue to live the questions together. The book's dialogical format shows that regenerative learning happens in the relationality between learner and educator and our capacity to constantly switch these roles."
– Dr. **Daniel Christian Wahl**, author of Designing Regenerative Culture, co-curator Executive Masters Regenerative Systems at ETH Zürich, co-host of the Regeneration Rising podcast and long-term contributor to the work of Gaia Education.

"Anyone who picks up this book expecting a how-to guide to regenerating higher education will be disappointed – which is a good thing, since following someone else's how-to or best practices list is the fastest way to extinguish the inner spirit that sources and sustains any truly regenerative path. Instead, the authors offer readers both an exploration and a manifestation of what they call "regenerative educatorship"– being in service to growing educators and education "that is designed from a position of deep care for the planet and all life in it." Perhaps most importantly, they point out that this is not and cannot be a mythic hero's journey. Rather, it is and must be "a journey of collective inquiry and purpose-focused community building." At a time when global division and othering are on the upswing, the role of educators and an education that remind us of our deep interdependence and of the unique gift each person can contribute if nurtured is vitally important."
– **Pamela Mang**, Co-founder and Education Program Manager of the Regenesis Institute for Regenerative Practice, Co-Author of Regenerative Design and Development.

"*The Art of Regenerative Educatorship* is a courageous inquiry into what it means to educate from a place of deep love, care, and reciprocity. Through a rich tapestry of personal reflections, shared dialogues, and real stories of innovative practice, the authors offer a vision for educating and learning that is both transformative and life-affirming. This book is a compelling invitation to reimagine education as a regenerative force, inspiring educators and learners alike to embark on a developmental journey of interconnection and meaningful change."
– Dr. **Nicholas Mang**, Core faculty and consultant at the Regenesis Institute for Regenerative Practice

"I was moved by the interwoven stories of these educators who are on a lively path of exploration and research. I deeply resonate with the aspiration of radically changing the way we view and relate to education, the spaces and systems that shape our perspective and our relationship to the world. It is remarkable how Mieke, Bas and Koen are firmly committed to their own development to be disruptive, deep and meaningful. Moreover, they have been fearless in undertaking this adventure towards regenerating educational systems and developmental conversations to regenerate the role of educators in the world."
– **Sidney Cano**, Economic Shaper, Cofounder & CIO at DUIT Corporation and Steward of the Regenerative Economy Communities (TREC)

"*The Art of Regenerative Educatorship* is a profound read for anyone engaged in challenging the dominant educational systems and paradigms. These are stories of emergence and adventure, yet most of all stories of nurturing new relationships. Highly recommended for its simplicity and sophistication."
– Dr. **Benjamin Freud**, Head of Upper School of Green School Bali and host of the Coconut Thinking Podcast

"This engaging and thought-provoking book serves as both a companion and guide, illuminating pathways into the emerging field of regenerative education. Blending the qualities of a guidebook with the warmth of a conversation among friends, it creates a reflective space for renewal and new learning. Original, engaging, and deeply informative, it's an essential resource for educators committed to this transformative field."
– Dr. **Richard Owens**, FRSA, Director, Woodleigh Institute, Regional Lead, Center for Systems Awareness

"In a world of exploitation, abuse of power and violence against ourselves and the Earth as a whole, it is easy to forget the enormous potential of living systems, natural intelligence and deep connections in forming a counter-hegemonic movement. *The Art of Regenerative Educatorship* not only reminds us of this potential, it also invites and enables educators from all walks of life to become part of a much needed regenerative force. A must read for educators in times of transition!"
- Prof. **Arjen Wals**, Professor of Transformative Learning for Socio-Ecological Sustainability and UNESCO Chair, Wageningen University

"This book is a profound invitation to reimagine education as a regenerative force – one that seeks to nurture not just learning, but life itself. Rather than offering a fixed model, it opens up a living, evolving conversation about the calling for an education that truly serves the well-being and flourishing of all life. A powerful and timely contribution that invites educators to step beyond habitual practices and into the art of regenerative educatorship. This book does not offer solutions – it enlivens and inspires meaningful inquiries. It is a gift to all educators seeking to cultivate deeper meaning, belonging, and wholeness"
- **Nuno da Silva**, Co-founder of Lúcida and faculty member of the Regenesis Institute for Regenerative Practice in Portugal

"This timely co-written book, looking at educational practices through the lens of regeneration, outlines viable alternatives to commercialisation and current financial cuts which impoverish education. Above all, it provides those with a heart for education with inspiration, resources and courage to continue their work, caring for the development of individuals and communities through the co-creation of sustainable learning environments."
- Prof. **Niki Vermeulen**, Professor in Science, Technology and Innovation Studies (STIS), University of Edinburgh, United Kingdom

"*The Art of Regenerative Educatorship* is an essential and timely invitation to reimagine education as a living system—one that nurtures the innate potential of individuals, communities, and the planet. More than just a book, this is a guide for transformation—providing essential pathways for evolving ourselves as educators, learners, and stewards of a regenerative future. With a deeply insightful and heart-centered approach, it bridges systemic change with personal evolution. A must-read for those ready to step into the future of education with courage, love, and purpose."
- Dr. **Anneloes Smitsman**, Founder & CEO of EARTHwise, award-winning co-author of the Future Humans Trilogy

"What is education for? In these turbulent times where crises abound and humanity appears not to be able to rise to the occasion, my mind keeps asking what is the role of education in this and how might we do education differently? This book is a beautiful tribute to how we can think differently about educatorship and how we can get closer to the essence of tuition. For the knowledge transfer focus of modern Western schooling does not prepare students for the turmoil of a disintegrating world. Because knowledge does not equal understanding and the knowledge transfer approach does not enable creative and courageous agency, a capability we now need more than ever. With this book, Mieke, Bas, and Koen take a bold step in reimagining the role of educators and they share helpful frameworks that can help you think differently too."
– Dr. **Leen Gorissen**, Innovation Biologist and Author

"*The Art of Regenerative Educatorship* is a timely book. It makes us look at and think about all things educational differently - regeneratively. The mutual resourcing throughout the book is so powerful that the resourcing co-evolves into something remarkably resourceful, the frameworks presented in these pages don't want to direct but want to free your thinking, and imaging is repeatedly used as a mental exercise to make an imaginative experience real. And as such we become privileged witnesses of what courage, presence, and love can accomplish throughout the whole educational system. In true regenerative spirit I wish to reciprocate that courage, presence, and love to Mieke, Bas, and Koen."
– **Robby Oblonsek**, Former School Director and Master of Science in Instructional and Educational Sciences

For Product Safety Concerns and Information please contact our EU
representative GPSR@taylorandfrancis.com
Taylor & Francis Verlag GmbH, Kaufingerstraße 24, 80331 München, Germany

www.ingramcontent.com/pod-product-compliance
Lightning Source LLC
Chambersburg PA
CBHW080250170426
43192CB00014BA/2625